Dear

Anxious

Christian

Lilly Horigan

Lilly Books
Bolivar, Ohio

Copyright © 2024 Lilly Horigan

Cover illustration copyright © 2024 by Lilly Horigan. All rights reserved.

Cover photo of threads copyright © 2024 NinaM/shutterstock.com. All rights reserved.

Scripture quotations, unless otherwise noted, are taken from The Holy Bible, New International Version®, NIV®. Copyright © 1973, 1978, 1984, 2011 by Biblica, Inc.®. Zondervan. All rights reserved worldwide.

Published by Lilly Books, LLC, PO Box 223, Bolivar, OH 44612

All rights reserved.

ISBN: 978-1-64683-008-4

No part of this publication may be reproduced.

This book is not intended to give specific medical, psychological, or emotional advice. Any person suffering from anxiety or depression should consult a doctor or licensed psychotherapist.

Contents

Introduction

1: Is My Anxiety a Disorder

2: Circumstantial Anxiety is Different

3: God Knows and Cares

4: Self-Reflection

5: Daily Living

6: Have a Talk with Yourself

7. Accepting the Less Than Perfect Days

8: Relationships

9: Positives of Anxiety

10: Anger

11: Study & Scriptures

12. My Anxiety Testimony

Word Find

References

Connect

About the Author

Other Books by Lilly

Introduction

Dear Anxious Christian,

You are not alone. When you're sitting at church and your tears continue to fall during worship, during the message, and while people filter out at the end; you are not alone. When you're hiding in your closet, refusing to go out, and unable to eat; you are not alone.

You believe with all your heart that you're a dedicated and "all in" Christ-follower, and you know that God is with you. That is a given. And somewhere deep down in your soul, you know others are suffering too. But that doesn't matter when you're in your own personal "pit of anxiety."

The people in your circle think you're failing to see the positive. Others think you're only focusing on the negative. People who've never experienced depression or anxiety think you have nothing to be anxious about because you live in a first world country and are rich compared to the rest of the world. But money and positivity don't lift you up out of that pit. Prayer keeps you from doing anything stupid like take your life, but you feel like you have no life. When you feel like that, you're not alone.

Your pastor says you've not made Christ the center of your life, your family says you're just being dramatic, and your friends think you need to stop labeling yourself as being anxious—that you're giving the devil a foothold by saying it out loud. And you fall deeper into the dark place. You read books by your favorite Bible teachers, you study books on cognitive therapy, and you journal your prayers. Nothing changes. Your spouse grows weary of it all. You're concerned you're screwing up your kids.

You feel like a failure.
Trust me: you are not alone.

My Hope

My hope is that this book helps you see that you're not less if you need something more. If you need medication, you're not a failure. If you need therapy, that's ok. If you need less stress than what you feel a "normal" person can handle, then do what you can to decrease your stress. I hope to share that we are all different, yet what we need to keep in common is remembering Who is in charge and Whose path we should be on.

> *Jesus said, "I am the way, the truth, and the life. No one comes to the Father except through me" (John 14:6).*

I won't be talking about the different types of anxiety disorders or medications in this book. There are tons of other resources that can offer up all the information you need. I try and only stick to the areas I understand and have experience with: Generalized Anxiety Disorder and generic Paxil (Paroxetine). And, of course, all the anxiety, worry, fear, guilt, and depression that comes with having anxiety—all while loving Jesus.

NOTE: My anxiety testimony is located in the final chapter. Please consider reading it first to better understand why I wrote this book in the first place. However, I understand we often buy a specific book for immediate help, and it can drive us crazy having to wait for it. Therefore, continue in whatever way works with my prayer that it is a blessing to you.

Pick a Way
(Copyright © 2008 Roxanne Timberlake, Album: All of Me, Artist: Timberlake Dawn.
Listen on all streaming websites.)

I know You're not the author of confusion.

That makes what I'm going through so very hard.

I'm praying I'll do what's right when it's all said and done.

That I listened to Your way in my heart.

And so I'll pick a way based on what You say.

I won't turn back I'll trust You to set me straight when I go the wrong way.

I know You'll reveal Your treasures to me that are hidden in Your Word for me to see.

I'm praying I'll obey so You can make known those treasures You've sent out of love.

And I know you're here, when I cannot feel You

You're here when I cannot see You. I know You're in control.

Oh and You're here, when I cannot feel You

You're here, when I cannot see You. I know you're in control every day. Every day.

I'll roll my works upon You, Lord.

Please make my thoughts all Yours.

That they agree, align with Your word.

You're my shield, my rock, my world.

~ Chapter 1 ~
Is My Anxiety a Disorder

To the Jews who had believed Him, Jesus said, "If you hold to my teaching, you are really my disciples. Then you will know the truth, and the truth will set you free" (John 8:31-32).

Dear Anxious Christian,

Some Christians find the idea of labeling a free ticket of power to Satan. That with the name of a disorder or disease, he receives the power to control and manipulate. I do not agree with that mindset. I believe he has more influence on our thoughts when we are confused, uncertain, and in the dark about what is going on in our world and bodies. But even that power has to be authorized by God. Remember, the first step in fixing a problem is identifying it. A label does not mean it is forever. It could even be wrong; but it does give us knowledge, steps, and guidance on how to move forward. All knowledge comes from God.

When I speak of my anxiety, I label it what it is: Generalized Anxiety Disorder (GAD).

While we all worry, what separates the individual with GAD from the average person is the intensity, frequency, and duration of his worrying. The GAD sufferer worries much more often, more intensely, and over a longer period of time. Worry becomes a way of

> *life and a damaging way of life at that (Hallowell, Worry).*

> *Usually [people with GAD] struggle with a large number of worries and spend a lot of time and energy doing it. The intensity and frequency of the worrying is always out of proportion to the actual problem (Anderson & Miller, Freedom from Fear).*

Naming my disorder helps me understand and work on the nuances of it, avoid my triggers, and improve in specific areas so that I can manage what is within my control while continuing to lift my anxiety and put it into God's hands. I don't give power to the name of my disorder. I hope to give all the power to God—He has it anyway.

Remember We Live in a Fallen World

In my book, *Does Everything Happen for a Reason, God?*, I detail how we have been born into a fallen world. If you don't know how it happened, I encourage you to get my book or a good study Bible and make sure you understand it. The Fall is why we are born beautiful in the eyes of God but broken in our spirits. Other than Jesus, nothing and no one on this Earth is perfect and the only thing that is good is God Himself. When we understand the Fall, we will be more patient with ourselves and others. We will have a greater appreciation for Christ's work on the cross and our salvation. We will understand the importance and process of sanctification (becoming more Christ-like).

Because we live in this fallen world, there are no guarantees that your baby will be born healthy or at all. There are no guarantees that your kids will outlive you and be healthy and wise. The one constant in a fallen world is that it is fair in its unfairness. All are on equal ground when it comes to living in a fallen world. No one can escape it. Of course, that is why Jesus—the Son of God—was born as we were born, lived in the same world we live in, but did it perfectly. His unjust death was the justification our world needed. Therefore, you are going to spend eternity somewhere. The choice of where is yours. If you have not made the choice to accept Christ as Lord, or do not understand His birth, life, death, and resurrection; choose now or seek wise, Christian counsel. Be sure to speak to someone who understands that Jesus was both man and God when He was on Earth and is part of the Trinity: God the Father, God the Son, and God the Holy Spirit.

You Are Not a Failure

> *Telling a person with GAD [Generalized Anxiety Disorder] to toughen up is like telling a person who has coronary artery disease that all he needs to do is unclog his coronary arteries (Hallowell,* Worry*)*

I constantly felt like a failure because I could not control my anxiety. When it got so bad that something had to be done, the feeling of failure was thick. Three days on generic Paxil helped me be the me I wanted to be. Admitting my "weakness" in controlling my anxiety on my own was the first step of months and years of greater emotional peace. *I was not less because I needed something more.* And if this need for medication was a weakness, then God was going to use it.

> ***But God chose the foolish things of the world to shame the wise; God chose the weak things of the world to shame the strong (1 Corinthians 1:27).***

Your feelings of failure may be ever present in your mind like they are in mine. Of course, God is with you in all these steps and ready for you to come to Him and talk about it. Having one or two people in your life that can lift you up when you are in those pits full of negative feelings is also very important. Sometimes you have to put effort into finding those people (like joining a Christ-centered recovery group such as Celebrate Recovery).

Remember, as long as you don't give up, and remind yourself that there is hope in every situation, you will never *be* a failure. You are not defined by the things you do or don't do, can or can't do; you are a precious creation of God and you will make mistakes and fall short because you live in a fallen world. Put your thoughts about failing into proper perspective. There is a purpose beyond what you can see and feel working within you.

Be Honest

I find it incredibly difficult to admit that I need help—even help given by God indirectly (through others or medication). Whatever it is that you struggle with about your anxiety or depression, you need to be honest with yourself, God, and a trusted individual. The stress of "trying" not to be anxious can take all the energy out of your life. Admitting the anger, the irritation, and the presence of your feelings is an important step. It is recognizing the problem, which is the first step to potentially solving it.

Your hatred of your own anxiety can be the shovel that digs you into a pit of depression. There is no balancing act you can completely do on your own between these two problems (anxiety and depression). It is Christ, at the center, who awaits to help you. And His ever present help may not be a cure-all. It could be years of process, but one that will be exponentially better than trying to do it on your own. You are casting your cares upon Him, which is what the Apostle Peter tells us to do (1 Peter 5:7).

When I am obsessing, magnifying, and catastrophizing, I am not functioning at my best level. I am trying to solve my problems in my own way.

> ***In their hearts humans plan their course, but the Lord establishes their steps (Proverbs 16:9).***

I am not oblivious of when I am trying to make things happen on my own, and the people around me can see it if they are paying attention. When I am in an anxious or stressed mode, I don't eat, sleep, relax, enjoy others, or even work well. I am almost useless unless I can throw myself in it to what it is I am worrying about. If I can solve or settle the matter, I can resolve the intense, anxious feelings. This requires me to know myself and my triggers.

Get Feedback

You know when you are struggling and the people around you probably know it too. Getting sound feedback from loved ones who know you well or counsel from a third party, can help immensely. Be mindful to talk to people who have given you sound advice in the past and/or have a solid relationship with Christ that is not legalistic. If you do not know who to talk to, consider professional therapy instead of advice.

> *Therapy differs from advice in that in therapy the patient gets involved in a process of discovery—discovery of new knowledge, techniques, feelings, connections, or insights—while advice, however wise, is just advice (Hallowell,* Worry*).*

But in the end, you must be honest with yourself about how you are doing. It's important to be aware that a lot of people may tell you there is nothing for you to worry or be anxious about. Unfortunately, I have found my anxiety to be no respecter of my income or possession level. These feelings and thoughts don't disappear at a certain salary. In fact, how often do we read in the news of some celebrity committing suicide?

Anxiety vs Worry

It seems the definitions of anxiety and worry differ depending on what you read or who you talk to. It often feels like the chicken or the egg debate. Which came first?

The Merriam-Webster dictionary states anxiety can be defined as an "apprehensive uneasiness or nervousness usually over an impending or anticipated ill. It can be a mentally distressing concern or interest. It stresses anguished uncertainty or fear of misfortune or failure."

Worry can be defined as "mental strangulation, being harassed with anxiety, to choke or strangle, to touch or disturb repeatedly, to torment, to struggle, to afflict with mental distress, agitation resulting from concern, or an incessant goading or attacking that drives one to desperation."

Dr. Edward M. Hallowell, in his book *Worry*, states: "Worry is a special form of fear. To create worry, humans elongate fear with anticipation and memory, expand it in imagination, and feel it with emotion."

He continues with a list of different types of worry:
- Adaptive worry: it alerts you to danger.
- Maladaptive worry: worry that serve no purpose and does more damage than good.

- Toxic worry: genetic worry that is inherited or a learned, deeply ingrained habit.
- Worry due to tragedies and trauma (I call this circumstantial worry).
- Habitual Worry: learned behavior.

J.P Moreland defines anxiety as a "feeling of uneasiness, apprehensions, or nervousness" in his book *Finding Quiet* and lists possible causes:
- Genetic predispositions.
- Parenting (controlling, overprotective).
- Early Childhood Experiences.
- Lifestyle (stress, trauma).
- Lack of control.

Samuel Johnson, an amazing man, who, in the 18th century, authored the first English dictionary and is considered one of the greats of English literature but who also battled a predisposition to anxiety and suffered from severe depression, defined his worry as "a desponding anticipation of misfortune, [that] fixes the mind upon scenes of gloom and melancholy, and makes fear predominate in the imagination."

The point is that we can quickly get confused with books, including the Bible sometimes, when it comes to worry and anxiety. But the bottom line that I hope to share is that there is some worry and anxiety that may be part of us and can be an opportunity or a stumbling block.

It's important to understand, process, and evaluate our anxiety/worry because the question of sin comes into play. I believe I have a bent toward anxiety that I was born with and my worry is what I try to do on my own to solve the anxiety. When I dwell in worry, it is a sign that I need to take it to God. When I embrace and hold onto the worry, I am now giving a door of opportunity to sin. The question of sin in regard to worry is one of the additional reasons for writing this book. Ultimately, I wanted to understand the heart of my anxiety, my predisposition toward it, and deal with it based on what God says, not man.

Is My Anxiety/Worry a Sin?

Ah...the question that plagues me. It is this question that I struggle with the most. I have had anxiety since I was four. Most of my family struggles with some type of mental illness, so when I read certain comments from spiritual leaders that seem to clump all anxiety and worry together I am even more confused. You can find words like the following with a simple search on the Internet about Christian anxiety:

- Worries cannot be blamed on a congenital condition.
- Worry is not something inherited by parents.
- Worry cannot be traced to genes.
- Worry cannot be excused.
- Worry is always sin.
- Worry is an action you choose.
- Worry is not trusting God.
- Worry is rebellion against God.

Why do these statements irritate me? It ignores the fallen condition of our world, which sickness is a part of. It ignores the improvement people experience with medication. When I have medicine that helps keep my serotonin at a balanced level, I am better at applying God's Word, casting my cares, and trusting Him.

After much study, I have come to the conclusion that sin comes into play when I let my circumstantial worry and anxiety have priority over my relationship with God by letting them have my entire focus and attention. In fact, in my research, I have found only one resource that I felt explained worry and anxiety (based on circumstances) as sin perfectly and understood that there is worry and anxiety that is not a sin and needs help:

> *Unlike normal anxiety, worry is not an involuntary physical response but a pattern we choose. Coming from within ourselves, it's a decision we make to stay in that place of anxiety, which was designed to protect us from immediate danger, not to see us through everyday life. For some, staying in a state of anxiety isn't a choice but, rather, a disorder that happens when the body's healthy, helpful biological process works overtime. An anxiety disorder is, essentially, too much of a good thing, afflicting 29 percent of us at some point in our life. It's very different from voluntary engagement in worry and requires treatment with medication, counseling, or both (Simpson, In Touch Ministries).*

Exactly! I can usually tell when I am choosing to worry and when I am battling anxiety. There is a difference. I cannot heal my anxiety, only God can do that via whatever way He sees fit, but I can reduce it with aid that He provides (utilizing methods I will share in this book). And voluntary worry is not something we can conquer all on our own either. It requires faith in God's compassion, faith in the Holy Spirit's work in our minds, and faith that He is a loving Father who cares for His children. Therefore, while I work on my anxiety with God's help because I recognize it as a disorder I must manage, I also work on reducing the voluntary worry in my life with

His help as well. I bring my whole heart (fears, worries, anxieties, anger) to Him.

Be Aware

I am always working on managing my anxiety. And being a perfectionist and a doer, I internally hope that with hard work I can conquer it. But that hard work leads to greater frustration, and what I should feel is satisfaction that I am taking responsibility for what is within my power and leaving the rest to God.

> *The problem is that [hard work] conquers a lot but it does not conquer all. Hard work does not conquer diabetes, nor does it change your height, nor will it remove a predisposition to anxiety. It can definitely help in the treatment—hard work is good for most problems—but it is not the cure (Hallowell,* Worry*).*

This is a great quote to keep in mind when reframing your human effort within your anxiety. Reframing is an excellent tool and method for having a paradigm shift (a change of view on how you see your anxiety and associated effort to manage it).

In my testimony in the final chapter, I share how I felt guilty being on medication because I was hearing messages from the pulpit that I needed to fully trust God for my healing. Not medication. This is dangerous preaching. Would we expect the same for someone with diabetes or heart disease? Would we tell them to not get help? God is the giver of knowledge. God has allowed medication to be created. The idea that medication for some things is fine but others is not, I believe, is allowing Satan to win. Obviously, not everything

God has allowed to be created is good for us. We live in a fallen world and people make horrible choices and creations with the knowledge they are given. But in this case, I think Satan wins when we don't encourage people to get the help they need and, instead, go around stating these all or nothing statements in our church family.

> *The weapons we fight with are not the weapons of the world. On the contrary, they have divine power to demolish strongholds. We demolish arguments and every pretension that sets itself up against the knowledge of God, and we take captive every thought to make it obedient to Christ (2 Corinthians 10:4-5).*

Statements like the following allow Satan to build strongholds within our lives and thoughts:
- You're just not having enough faith in God.
- You're not putting God first in your life.
- You're not handing it all over to God.
- You're not praying hard or long enough.
- It's all in your head...

Thankfully, there is only one thing we need to do and remember when it comes to pleasing God: believe! Not stop thinking and believe. Not stop worrying and believe. Not stop crying and believe. Just believe.

> *Overhearing what they said, Jesus told him, "Don't be afraid; just believe" (Mark 5:36).*

~ Chapter 2 ~
Circumstantial Anxiety is Different

Dear Anxious Christian,

If you have received confirmation in your heart or by a doctor that your anxiety is neurological, then you may soon learn—or already know—the difference between the neurological anxiousness and the circumstantial anxiety in your life.

For example, there is a baseline anxiety that I have always felt. That baseline is adjusted up or down depending if I am on medication and according to the impact of stress in my life.

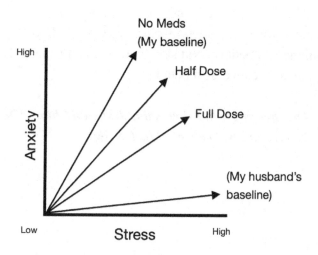

My baseline anxiety is also impacted by how much of the medication I am on.

When circumstantial anxiety increases it requires extra effort in handing it over to God. This is when we need to be even more diligent with prayer, thanksgiving, and supplication as Paul states in Philippians 4 because rolling it over and over in our head is going to move us into trying to solve it on our own. When this happens in my life, I increase my time with God each day, get together with my sponsor, and immerse myself in God's Word via reading, sermons, podcasts, etc.

This is all back to knowing yourself and maintaining your intimate relationship with the Father. Everyone is different. I doubt my husband would know how to be truly anxious. He was gifted with an exuberant amount of self-control, patience, and the natural ability to reframe. He doesn't question "why" and, instead, trusts that God has allowed it for a reason. Therefore, it is hard for him to understand my anxiety. We have now been together for over twenty years and all the years have been necessary for understanding one another to the best of our ability.

Having a friend or two who understands your anxiety disorder is crucial. They should encourage but not enable. They should be honest but not try to change the basis of your spirit. They should be discerning but not condemning. You will know who these people are when you find them. It is important to put yourself in places where you can find these people: church, Christ-centered recovery programs, and small groups.

When you find your anxiety is based on circumstances outside of your control, that is when you take the steps of peace that work for you—keeping God's Word in mind. This could be through conversations, prayer, journaling, praise, and even movies or books that remind you of God's sovereignty. Our Father is creative, and we are too. Don't limit your peace process to a one size fits all. (Only be sure not to include anything that is against God's Will and Word for you: drunkenness, illegal drugs, extramarital affairs, porn, etc.)

Past

Recovery programs are helpful to determine if your anxiety is a learned behavior from some past event(s). Often it is when we can sit down and open up with others that we discover we are the way we are in some aspects because of events of our past. When I began attending Celebrate Recovery, I did so for my anxiety and anger. However, while completing the 12-step program with a great group of women, I discovered much of my circumstantial anxiety was due problems with my relationship with my mother.

Our hearts may hold untold, deeper reasons for our circumstantial worry and anxiety. Take your past to God and ask Him to show you any areas of hurt that have not been dealt with yet.

Do Your Part

Whatever your circumstantial anxiety looks like, I recommend you do everything in your power/control to "clean up" whatever may be, or has the possibility of, making your anxiety worse. For example, if you are cheating on your taxes, this is going to create an internal anxiety and may become an external anxiety when it becomes known. Or perhaps your health is getting worse and the cause is eluding your doctors, but you know you are drinking excessive amounts of alcohol, eating horrible food, or not exercising at all. Maybe you have not forgiven someone in your life and God's trying to get you to notice it.

God will use circumstantial anxiety to get our attention. It may be true that what is going on has nothing to do with your own actions and is due to an attack by Satan, the fact we live in a fallen world, a test of our faith, or God is allowing it for a purpose that you will never know or fully understand; but we must honestly evaluate ourselves. Nothing is hidden from God.

Ask Him if you have opened the door to the circumstantial anxiety you are feeling. If He brings something to your attention, begin to fix it. It is also very possible that there is a weakness or an area in your life God is working on in you which is not a sin at all; therefore, others might not understand the problem you have with that issue. But if you think about your relationship with Christ as a multi-level game/course then working on issues, even those that are not sin, makes sense.

To get in the game or course, you must accept Christ and you start at level one. But as time advances, growth occurs and tests are passed that advance you to harder levels/courses. I know that in my own home, what bothers me right now while watching TV is not what bothers my husband (and definitely does not bother my adult son). Even within the same home, we are at different levels in our walk with Christ. That is a small example, but the concept can be applied to all kinds of areas.

Do not be deceived: God cannot be mocked. A man reaps what he sows (Galatians 6:7).

Let us not become weary in doing good, for at the proper time we will reap a harvest if we do not give up (Galatians 6:9).

Bottom line: Don't do the things you know will bring more anxiety! Aim to be righteous in all your endeavors and listen when God is showing you sin and areas of temptation in your life.

Cast your cares on the Lord and He will sustain you; He will never let the righteous be shaken (Psalm 55:22).

God's Ultimately in Control

God's ultimately in control, and we need to trust Him and His timing. He doesn't answer to anyone. He can do what He wants within His nature and has purposes and goals that we probably will never see. We can trust Him. Maybe what you're going through seems unfair. Remember, God doesn't answer to you and His grace is always sufficient.

Therefore God has mercy on whom He wants to have mercy, and He hardens whom He wants to harden (Romans 9:18).

Gratitude

I will remember the deeds of the Lord; yes, I will remember your miracles of long ago (Psalm 77:11).

Thanking God is an important part of our walk through this life and it's easy to not see all the amazing things going on when our anxiety is magnified. One of our goals can include glorifying God more than our situations. We can always find something to be thankful for in our day, even if it is the simple fact that our hearts are still beating and we're still breathing.

Find a way to add gratitude to your day. I use a gratitude list before bed (usually just 5 things right after I complete a TA-DA list of 5 things I got done that day as well). I also journal my gratitude every few days by listing out anything I can think of at that time.

We can be thankful that, with Jesus, there is always an answer to everything that is going on in our lives. He will never leave us. He is in control and knows what we can endure. Gratitude helps us take our minds off ourselves and the events going on around us so we can put our focus on Him. Gratitude also helps increase our trust and it's an important part of lifting our anxiety to God.

__Do not be anxious about anything, but in every situation, by prayer and petition, with thanksgiving, present your requests to God (Philippians 4:6).__

We can choose to focus our thoughts on the truth that God's got us! When fear, worry, and that above baseline anxiety begins to consume us, we can be thankful that He still loves us. In fact, when we set our minds on His perfect love, fear naturally dissipates. Maybe not as fast as we would like, but it can't help but reduce:

__There is no fear in love. But perfect love drives out fear, because fear has to do with punishment. The one who fears is not made perfect in love (1 John 4:18).__

God always cares, and He is working in us. He is not angry and is blessing our actions to put Him first. Parents love it when their kids come to them and admit they are struggling with something and can use assistance. Good parents don't throw those kids out, tell them to suck it up, or to deal with it on their own. Our Heavenly Father is a good, good Father.

We may not think of ourselves as ungrateful, but if we have a heart that refuses to be satisfied, then we are having a heart of ingratitude. Ingratitude can also look like pride and being overly focused on ourselves. This is an area that I struggle to balance since I am very self-focused. I am a lifelong learner and am always trying to improve, to be where God wants me, and to use my skills in a way that will be advantageous to the Kingdom. I can easily take my goal for Kingdom work and make it so self-focused that it ends in a pity-party. Be mindful of your satisfaction. It can be a very good indicator of your gratitude level.

Prayer

Philippians 4:6 mentions prayer before anything else when it comes to anxiety and circumstances. Prayer is a privilege. Going to God first, even before your friends and family, is vital. It's not a rule or a requirement, but it helps to remember that He is in control. Going to social media first and seeing what your friends think, or going to search engines and getting what experts, think is not wrong. Nor do I think God gets mad at us when we go to someone else before Him, but being mindful of our steps in our anxiety is helpful and important.

In prayer, we give God the opportunity to reach us in our thoughts and give Him time and space for His revelation. His Word reminds us of the power of our prayers when lifted in faith into His hands:

> ***Therefore I tell you, whatever you ask for in prayer, believe that you have received it, and it will be yours (Mark 11:24).***

Thankfully, God knows what we need before we lift any prayer to Him, but it is important to also be clear in our prayers. In this way, we are not only being honest with ourselves and God, but it gives God an opportunity to speak into our spirit— guiding us into a specific action for that specific prayer or simply a revelation about the prayer request. Remember Philippians 4:6 talks about "definite requests."

For my busy and active mind, I do much better journaling my prayers. It helps me be more specific about each prayer. My mind wanders so easily that I can get distracted when speaking or thinking them. However, singing my prayers is something that also helps tremendously. In the car, when journaling is not an option, I might visualize Jesus in the passenger seat (ironic, since He is the Captain of my life), and I just speak to Him the way I would a friend. Find what works and do it.

Prayer helps us be honest with God about what we are feeling. It puts us into our rightful place: a small but important part of His creation. It leads us to right action, forgiveness, and awareness of our future when we stand before Him. It reminds us that we are not alone, and He is our strength.

~ Chapter 3 ~
God Knows and Cares

For we do not have a high priest who is unable to empathize with our weaknesses, but we have one who has been tempted in every way, just as we are—yet He did not sin. Let us then approach God's throne of grace with confidence, so that we may receive mercy and find grace to help us in our time of need (Hebrews 4:15-16).

Dear Anxious Christian,

I am so glad that God is there for us in our emergencies, but I'm even happier that He is in our life at every moment. He walks with us in the good and the bad. The happy and the sad. The fun and the confused. He is a loving, loving Father who holds us in all moments—including the anxious ones.

Anxiety weighs down the heart, but a kind word cheers it up (Proverbs 12:25).

Psalm 6 is an excellent resource to help you remember the truth in your anxieties. God knows:
- Your weaknesses
- When you're hurting
- When your body is aching
- When your soul is greatly troubled
- How long your troubles will last

- The extent of your weariness
- Why you are complaining
- Why you throw pity parties
- The reason for your tears
- The depth of your wails
- The intensity and authenticity of your prayers

One of the amazing aspects of our heavenly Father is that He receives it *all*. He does not shoo us away like some annoying fly. No good parent does that to their children. And God is good. In fact, He alone is all that is good in this world. When we see good, it is Him. When we see beauty, it is Him.

Don't be ashamed of your hurts, anxieties, and worries. If you are taking them to Him in honesty, and with the intention of lifting them up to Him for His wisdom and guidance, then, in my opinion, you are not sinning— you are growing.

Remember, it is in the dwelling, accepting, and not fighting our worry where sin comes in. It's in the giving into it and not doing what you can to tackle it (changing thoughts, reframing, prayer, etc.). It's in the lack of lifting it to Christ and not recognizing that He alone is sustainer, comforter, and designer of all things. That is when worry will become sin: when it becomes your precious and you do nothing to move forward. God rewards our diligence, understands our anxieties, and He comforts us.

When anxiety was great within me, your consolation brought me joy (Psalm 94:19).

Keep reading. You're moving forward.

Confusion

I have already written about the confusion I have concerning sin when I read some Christian books on anxiety. Add to it comments such as these, and the confusion increases:
- Worriers are hypocrites.
- People who bear the cross have no worry.
- True Christ-followers alway have peace for their mind is on Christ.
- Positive thinking is not part of the solution to worry.
- Positive thinking leads one to believe they can solve the problem of worry on their own.
- Peace only comes when properly aligned with Christ.

So, we can't banish all worry or anxiety on our own (I agree), but what if we still worry and have accepted Christ as our Lord and Savior? Are we just utter Christian failures and fooling ourselves? I had a pastor tell me that if I am worrying then I am not putting Christ at the center of my life. Well, that just blew my mind. I was so upset and sad when I heard those comments. God's Word states:

Who are you to judge someone else's servant? To their own master, servants stand or fall. And they will stand, for the Lord is able to make them stand (Romans 14:4).

It is to God who I go to first and who will judge me. How can we say such all or nothing statements to each other—as if we understand everything that is going on in our brains, the results of trauma earlier in life, our intimate relationship with Christ, etc.

Why do you look at the speck of sawdust in your brother's eye and pay no attention to the plank in your own eye? How can you say to your brother, 'Let me take the speck out of your eye,' when all the time there is a plank in your own eye? You hypocrite, first take the plank out of your own eye, and then you will see clearly to remove the speck from your brother's eye (Matthew 7:3-5).

One of my goals for this book is to bring hope to my fellow Christ-followers who struggle to understand their anxiety. I only point out my own frustration to encourage young to share that you are not alone if you don't understand or struggle to reconcile statements you hear. Nowhere in the Bible have I found where God Himself makes me feel like such a failure. He tells me to not fear, to not worry, to not be anxious; but He never tells me I don't love Him, or am failing to put Him first, when I struggle with these things.

Christ-followers are part of God's family and each one has weaknesses. Each one answers to God; therefore, we need to be careful not to judge each other in a critical way.

There are many Christian books on the market that state you shouldn't worry. That you can't blame your genes or a chemical imbalance. That you're a hypocrite because you're not trusting God. And then, when the authors have made you feel completely condemned about something out of your control if you have an anxiety disorder, they proceed to try and help you to not worry. My husband tells me books such as these, and most of the sermons we hear about anxiety, are for the "normal" person who does not have struggle with an anxiety disorder.

But not all books and sermons that deal with anxiety in a Christian's life leave the reader with hopelessness and frustration. *Freedom from Fear: Overcoming Worry & Anxiety* by Neil Anderson and Rich Miller does an excellent job of discussing all aspects of anxiety in an encouraging manner: "Peace is the antithesis of anxiety. If you desire peace, you have to pursue the Prince of Peace and earn to live a responsible life dependent upon Him. You can't just do away with anxiety; you *overcome* when you abide in Christ."

Remember, there is a level of worry that is sin. But if you love Christ and you want to work on reducing all your anxiety/worry (that which is in and out of your control), you are in the right place and you are not alone. God knows and cares about you and your struggles.

> ***Be kind and compassionate to one another, forgiving each other, just as in Christ God forgave you (Ephesians 4:32).***

If while reading books and listening to sermons you recognize all or nothing type of statements about your faith and your anxiety, try not to get angry, depressed, or more anxious by these comments. Take the good of the resource and ignore the rest. Stay in God's Word as much as possible. There is hope in it. (Unfortunately, I have read some amazing Christian books on anxiety only to later discover that some of the writers were also on medication for anxiety but never mention it in their own book! I think this does a disservice to the reader.)

In regard to those all or nothing statements we hear, remember that God is the only one who can accurately judge us. Our actions. Our thoughts. Our sins. We must be careful to not try and be God in other people's lives and not allow someone else to be God in ours. Our hope must rest in Christ.

Do not give up hope—hope of healing, improving, and using what is happening in your life for God. Don't let any past or present failures leave you hopeless about your future. You're not a failure because you struggle. Hating your "anxious" self does no good. God is probably using it in a way you may never see this side of heaven.

Challenges

Do you have a hard time understanding hope or seeing it in your circumstances? Remember, Jesus is available to you in all things. We may not understand everything as we go through it, but we can be sure that He's with us in all of our difficult circumstances. Just make sure that your relationship with Him is thriving (not just on Sunday morning for an hour).

I can do all this through Him who gives me strength (Philippians 4:13).

As we live our life for God, our path and purpose are made evident. Enjoying the journey we are on is part of our destiny. Even the seasons of pain, disappointment, and confusion are full of change and surprise. God is always doing something unexpected in our lives because He sees all angles and moments. And when we use our pain to help others, as I hope this book is helping you, it puts a dent in the goals of the devil.

Do not be overcome by evil, but overcome evil with good (Romans 12:21).

When we feel alone in our walk, we can trust and lean on God's guidance to redirect us if/when we get off track. Each path, season of hardship, and areas that trip us up are ways we fulfill our purpose. With these challenges, we experience blessings and learn new things. God is always leading us to move forward, not backtrack through the pain. It is in the hard seasons that we grow—just as trees strengthen via the wind.

When going through any challenge, consider your view of Jesus. Your view of Him will impact every aspect of your life. He is the one who transforms you. Is He becoming greater and greater in your life while you become less and less? He is always working for our good (because we love Him), and our hope in Him equals greater faith *through* our challenges. You will gain confidence and joy the more you place challenges in His hands. It is impossible to have a lifelong fellowship with God and not have more joy in your life. Your joy may not be where you want it, but as long as your view of Jesus is rooted in right thinking, increased joy will be the result.

Works in Progress

Why are we Christ-followers? Because we know we are all fallen creatures who need a perfect Savior to be the propitiation for our sin. When we accepted Christ as Lord, we received salvation. But we did not become fully Christ-like. That process is called sanctification and it is what we should spend the rest of our life pursuing.

God knows we struggle with anxiety. True, He could heal us immediately if He wanted to and I do ask for that. But God has purpose in everything. We can be confident He has purpose in how we were made and what makes us tick at this moment.

I like to think of my life as a tapestry. I am a masterpiece of God's work. But when the back of my "tapestry" is seen, it looks pretty messy. There are "stops" and "starts" of threads. There are crisscrosses, knots, and a bit of chaos. I tend to focus on the look of the back of this masterpiece called life and not the front. And we do tend to understand life backwards.

However, maybe this can be a moment where you remember that you're not the Creator. You're not the Master of your own masterpiece. You are the assistant doing what your Master is leading you to do (hopefully). And when we trust Him with every aspect of ourselves, we can be sure the masterpiece of our life will be purposeful and beautiful according to His desires.

So, don't give up. Press on. Bring all your anxiety to Him, listen to His promptings, and do what you can as His assistant to live *with Him* in control and not your anxiety. He loves you. He is not mad at you for needing medication. He is not mad at you when the little things feel overwhelming. He is a wonderful Father that wants to hold your hand through all things.

Perfection

> ***Be perfect, therefore, as your heavenly Father is perfect (Matthew 5:48).***

God demands perfection but He understands it can only happen with Him through Christ. Never on our own. God will only be satisfied with perfection in His house (which we'll have in heaven because we put our faith in Jesus), but He is thrilled to see His children put effort into each step in their walk with Him. In Christ, we are perfectly covered. God also uses our life here on earth to perfect our spirit—our sufferings, our hurts, our habits—to improve us on our way to His home.

Failures in perfection, or even that God calls us to it, should not discourage us, but encourage us instead. It gives us hope of improvement, and it reminds us of God's grace and His gift of Christ—a gift we did not deserve. We need to think of perfection as a process of growing more spiritually mature. God is looking at our heart!

See yourself as a daughter or son of God and have a talk with Him about it. Watch Him respond with, "You made a mistake but you brought it to me, and together we can more forward and use it for knowledge."

> *Not that I have already obtained all this, or have already arrived at my goal, but I press on to take hold of that for which Christ Jesus took hold of me. Brothers and sisters, I do not consider myself yet to have taken hold of it. But one thing I do: Forgetting what is behind and straining toward what is ahead, I press on toward the goal to win the prize for which God has called me heavenward in Christ Jesus (Philippians 3:12-14).*

Remember Where your Help Comes From

Psalm 88 is an excellent example in God's Word of how we may be feeling in our daily battle with anxiety: depressed with a lack of hope. In this psalm we may find understanding, as the Psalmist speaks of his troubles, how he feels close to dying, his depression, and his terrors.

> *For my soul is full of troubles, and my life draws near to the grave. I am counted with those who go down to the pit; I am like a man who has no strength (Psalm 88: 3-4).*

The key to this psalm, and the example we need to walk away with, is that the Psalmist's faith is evident. He brings his hurts to the only One in the world Who understands him and can help him. We must do the same. Even when we don't understand what is going on, we need to trust God and bring it all to Him. He is the only one in control over everything. It would be foolish not to go to Him in our joy and our pain. Ironically, it is usually in our joy we fail to go to God.

I struggled with anxiety for 24 years without Christ, and, although I understand more than I did then, I am still very confused at times about why I struggle with what others seem to have no problem handling. But the 22 years of anxiety I have had with Christ, which He knows about and understands, is better than any day without Him. I'm not walking alone in my anxiety and He understands my soul (my mind, will, and emotions). He understands every thought, fear, hurt, and hope. My faith is evident in that I come to Him about it all. It would be foolish for me to do anything less, even if I still walk away not understanding. I will trust the one who understands everything.

Jesus looked at them and said, "With man this is impossible, but with God all things are possible." (Matthew 19:26).

It is clear, that with God all things are possible and everything would be worse without Him. Studies show that people of faith are three times more likely to survive open-heart surgery than those of no faith (Hallowell). Rates of depression and sickness due to anxiety are lower in people of faith, and those who attend church regularly have a 50% less chance of dying of coronary-heart disease. Therefore, hanging onto faith in Christ is the most important thing to do with all the anxiety, circumstances, and thoughts in our lives. Don't give up on giving it *all* over to God's *all*-knowing, *all*-powerful hands.

A Healthy Mind

I think a healthy mind looks different for everyone in this fallen world. An unhealthy mind does impact our health and relationships, but knowing what a "healthy/balanced" mind looks like for ourselves is important in walking through this life. God is on our side and is in complete control, but we need to keep a hold of Him through it all.

Have you ever seen teachers leading children down the road with a long rope that everyone is holding? The teacher is leading these kids safely through a chaotic environment and as long as the kids keep a hold of the rope, all will go well. Life is like a crazy, obstacle course. Jesus is at the head of that rope, but we have to HOLD ON!

Do not be wise in your own eyes; fear the Lord and shun evil (Proverbs 3:7).

Finding specific and personal ways to help keep your mind healthy and balanced is important. Of course, everyone needs to be in God's Word consistently, worshiping, praising, and praying. Keeping a journal and reminding yourself of all the blessings in your life is also important.

Finally, brothers and sisters, whatever is true, whatever is noble, whatever is right, whatever is pure, whatever is lovely, whatever is admirable—if anything is excellent or praiseworthy—think about such things. Whatever you have learned or received or heard from me, or seen in me—put it into practice. And the God of peace will be with you (Philippians 4:8-9).

What is true in your life? What is noble? Just? Pure? Lovely? Write and think on these things.

~ Chapter 4 ~
Self-Reflection

Dear Anxious Christian,

How do you feel about *you*?' Do you think about your nature and personality? Does it bring you joy or irritation? Have you taken the personality quizzes only to be irritated with the results? Are you the 'you' you want to be? Or are you constantly jealous when you see those qualities come so easily and naturally in someone else?

For years, I tried hard to change my nature and personality. I was (still am, of course) a classic Type A personality. I'm also a perfectionist, very analytical, lean toward the negative, and able to magnify anything to the point of detriment. I tried hard to change those areas so that I could be a better *me* in Christ.

C. S. Lewis wrote, "It is when I turn to Christ, when I give myself up to his personality, that I first begin to have a real personality of my own" *(Mere Christianity)*. I tried so hard not to be the me I was that I missed what God was doing. As I turned more of myself over to Christ, God was able to continually mold me into the true 'me' that He designed me to be.

Lewis explains the importance of getting yourself out of the way in his book *Mere Christianity*. For example, he stated, "As long as your own personality is what you are bothering about, you are not going to Him at all. Your real, new self will not come when you are looking for it. It comes when you are looking for Him."

This is what happened for me. Once I stopped focusing on changing the nature of myself—which was impossible and frustrating—and instead focused on Christ and His work within me, I was able to see the purpose in how God created me.

If I didn't have my personality, I wouldn't be where I am today. I wouldn't be doing the things He has asked me to do. The strengths of my personality—how God invented me—are what He is using to fulfill His purpose in my life. Many of the tasks required in my work require my exact personality: detailed, precise, analytical, focused.

What do you detest about your personality? Now try and think of a purposeful way God used it to place you where you are in your life right now. What we see as annoying personality traits are most likely exactly what we need to fulfill our purpose. It's almost like God knew what He was doing when He created us—wink, wink! Let's trust that and not fight against the current.

Guilt

When I am not the "me" I want to be, or the "me" someone says I should be, the emotion of guilt arises. I attended a church for many years where I heard the pastor state that if one just dealt with any guilt, then one could get off medication. Well, that just made me feel guiltier—if I felt I was struggling with guilt at all before I heard it.

If guilt is the cause of some worry, I am sure God's Word is going to show us where that guilt is hidden when we dedicate time and effort into reading it. But I have to disagree with putting all the fault of worry or anxiety onto guilt. There is a plethora of other non-medical causes of anxiety: loneliness, pain, fear, abuse, etc. I feel we do a disservice to the Christian community when we try and pigeonhole one entire feeling with another.

In fact, perhaps it is an attack that God has allowed the enemy to take in order to refocus and examine us. Anxiety and worry attack our minds and they can distract us from what God wants us to do, so they should be triggers for going to God in that moment. Perhaps they are also reactions to something we are feeling or missing in our life that we can't pinpoint. This is where monitoring and logging is important. Taking note of when feelings "hit" can help define the triggers and the underlying feelings they may be hiding.

Sometimes my moments of severe anxiety are the opportunities I need to reach out to someone in kindness—it removes me from my problem, letting me be a blessing to others.

Frustration

Obviously, worry is a huge problem in our society. Within a Christian, it can be a huge frustration. Worry and anxiety can make us literally sick in so many different ways. We worry about its sinfulness and our inability to fight it. Paul says the answer is not to be anxious about anything, which can make the anxious Christian more…anxious. Thankfully, we can bring our anxiety, and our anxiety about our anxiety, to God. It is the ultimate action step so that we don't dwell in it:

> ***Do not be anxious about anything, but in every situation, by prayer and petition, with thanksgiving, present your requests to God (Philippians 4:6).***

God is aware of what we struggle with in our daily lives. He's aware of our fears, worries, hopes, and dreams. We need not hide from Him. We can bring Him everything we are thinking. Nothing is too small. Prayer shows that we are dependent on Him, that we are leaning on Him. Does it make

God angry when we repeat our prayer? No, that is why Paul reminds us to "petition." We are to do it over and over again if we find we are taking it back onto ourselves and letting it hinder and weigh us down. Then we give thanks that He hears us and that God's perfect action will take place—whatever it may be.

We ask for what He wants us to have. We ask for what He believes we need for the moment we are in. I have prayed repeatedly that God would take my anxiety disorder away. The answer has been no so far. I must trust that He is using this for my good and to not let my frustration trump the beauty that is God's sovereignty.

Thankfully, I never have to be frustrated about God listening to me—He always does. I never need to be frustrated that I am not strong enough to endure the situation I'm going through—I can handle it with His strength. And I never need to be frustrated that God is not interested—I am always able to lift my cares up to Him because He loves me. You can say the same, my fellow sibling in Christ.

God perfects His work in us and will continue to do so until Christ's return. We don't have to hate ourselves because of our weaknesses. We can love ourselves in each moment of growth because God is in us. God doesn't just flow and work through "perfect" people. He shines through the brokenness within us and uses it to help others if we let Him. Learn to love yourself as God loves you.

Insecurity, anxiety, and depression are incredibly common in our society, and much of this is due to self-judgement, to beating ourselves up when we feel we aren't winning in the game of life (Neff, Self-Compassion*).*

Note: Some people may use chapter four of Philippians to make Christians feel guilty, ashamed, or weak in their faith. Some Christians believe that you should hear Philippians 4 and your anxiety should just go away. Be mindful when people are trying to use this chapter to make you think there is something wrong with you. And be honest: are you beating yourself up with Philippians 4?

Peace

> ***Jesus said, "I have told you these things, so that in me you may have peace. In this world you will have trouble. But take heart! I have overcome the world" (John 16:33).***

God knows we struggle and that all peace will come only from pausing and relaxing in our acknowledgment of His sovereignty in our lives. But do not be fooled into thinking that this peace should be automatic or easy. For some, it may be. I hear stories of people coming to Christ and the peace they have felt is overwhelming and lasting. However, for most, this is not the case.

I always felt like a failure because I still lacked the peace I sought as I did my best to rest in God's awesomeness. There is no way to know how worse I would be had I not even tried. *I know* I am growing and improving in this journey, and *I am* thankful for that. I just need to ignore the preaching that states that if I still struggle with peace, faith, anxiety, worry, etc.; that I am not a true Christ-follower. That is an all or nothing statement that I believe hinders the progress we are making in our walk with the Lord. I know I need to ignore the comments that I am not trusting God enough, that I shouldn't need meds, or it's all in my head. I hope my struggle with such comments will help you be more mindful when you hear them as well.

As long as anxious Christians follow God's Word and believe that God is at work within them for His good, I know improvement is going to happen. Purpose is going to be realized through the process.

> *And the peace of God, which transcends all understanding, will guard your hearts and your minds in Christ Jesus (Philippians 4:7).*

Fear of Rejection and Failure

Who do you fear will reject you? Is it God? He sees your heart. He sees your faith. He will not leave you nor forsake you. Do you fear others will not accept you and hurt you? Give it over to God. I received more rejection in my life when I accepted Christ than any other decision I ever made. Not everyone is going to approve of your decisions. It's only following God's direction in your life that matters.

> *Fear of man will prove to be a snare, but whoever trusts in the Lord is kept safe (Proverbs 29:25).*

Ironically, when we fear rejection, we often behave in a way that will make people reject us. Be mindful of who you are trying to please. Ask God for favor with people. When people mistreat you, God takes it personally. God will replace the people who hate you with others who will build you up in your faith. Shake the rejection off and trust God.

> *Do not fear, Zion; do not let your hands hang limp. The Lord your God is with you, the Mighty Warrior who saves (Zephaniah 3:16b-17).*

Fear of failure is probably one of the biggest fears for anxious Christians. I constantly feel like a failure that I can't be more peaceful, more faithful, more trusting, less worried, etc. I do find comfort in the Apostle Paul. He did things he didn't want to do. He struggled.

No one ever says Paul didn't trust God or that he was a failure. He brought it to God and he shared his struggles with his brothers and sisters in Christ. He is an example of being honest, pressing on, and fulfilling the purpose God gave him with and through his weaknesses.

Fear Things Will Never Change

Perhaps God leaves something imperfect in us so we can lean on Him. In 2 Corinthians, Paul had a "thorn in the flesh" which he asked to have removed but God said no. It doesn't matter what the thorn was...it bothered him.

> *Being confident of this, that He who began a good work in you will carry it on to completion until the day of Christ Jesus (Philippians 1:6).*

Maybe our anxiety will never be gone this side of heaven. But we can be in a state of recovery and hope when it comes to our anxiety and in a state of excitement for what God is doing with it at the same time. We can only change what is in our power to change, and we must give the rest to God. He is not oblivious of our hurts. We can come boldly to Him and ask for healing, and we can ask Him for strength to endure the suffering with a good attitude. We can live in hopeful expectation when we have put Him first and lean on Him continually.

Is Jesus Really First in Your Life?

Our days are filled with important and sometimes urgent events. It's important that we get up and go to school or go to work. It's important the family has food, shelter, and clothing. For some, these things are urgent. It's important the bills are paid on time and it's urgent when they are not. It's important we go to the doctor and sometimes that care is needed urgently. It's important we spend time with others. It's important we believe in Jesus, go to church, and work toward our purpose.

But there is one thing in our lives that should be more important, more prominent—meaning it should be PREEMINENT—and that is putting Jesus first in our lives. The Apostle Paul stated in Colossians that all things were created by Jesus. All that is in heaven and on earth. All thrones and dominions. Jesus created all things and through Him all things exist. Therefore, Paul tells us that Jesus is preeminent. He is first in everything we see and don't see.

When Jesus is preeminent in our hearts, He will be first in our jobs, our homes, our habits, our activities, our social calendars. He will be our North Star, our focal point. So, is Jesus important in your life or is He preeminent?

And why should Jesus be first in our lives? As believers, we know we're going to spend eternity somewhere and that somewhere is settled because of what Jesus did and our choice to make Him our Lord and Savior. The Apostle Peter says Jesus is at the right hand of God and that all authorities and powers are subject to Him. Therefore, it is wise to make Jesus first, since He is in control of it all anyway. Paul reminds us in Colossians that in Christ are hidden all the treasures of wisdom and knowledge—another reason to make Jesus first.

Jesus Himself tells us in Matthew that we are to seek first the kingdom of God. Who is the head of the kingdom of God?

Jesus. When you recognize Jesus as your king, you'll understand that the king doesn't want to be an important/prominent part of your life. He wants to be the priority in it. Society is not going to look at you strangely when you think Jesus is an important man, a good teacher, or a wise prophet. Society doesn't usually make fun of the occasional or even weekly church attender. And in America, most won't think you're too weird if you believe Jesus is God's Son and that He died on a cross and rose again. Society is ok with Jesus being important. But when He is preeminent in your time, talent, and treasure, then society thinks you're off your rocker.

> *For where your treasure is, there your heart will be also (Matthew 6:21).*

When Jesus is preeminent, you see it in your bank account. When Jesus is preeminent, you see it in your schedule. When Jesus is preeminent, you see it in how you treat yourself and others. Today, evaluate your priorities and see if Jesus is prominent or preeminent in your life. This is a vital reflection step in your battle with anxiety. Making Jesus first won't necessarily make the anxiety go away, but he will be with us through it.

Activities

Are you doing the things you enjoy when you struggle? Or does it all stop? This can be a good indicator of how things are going for you. The problem I find with my anxiety is that my creative and talented side slows down to nothing and the longer I do nothing, the harder it is to start up again. Having an accountability partner to encourage you helps immensely.

Scheduling activities in advance is a good way to get out of your head as well and get you motivated.

> *Uplifting words may not solve a problem, but the temporary relief helps the discouraged one endure the struggle longer (Chuck Swindoll).*

One of the biggest areas of improvement in my mental health has been being part of a local, Christian support group. It's easy to just stay at home and not do anything, especially if your anxiety is increased in social activities, but being active is good for you. When we stay home, we can easily fall into addictive behavior, laziness, and procrastination. Having everything streamed on our devices doesn't help. Ironically, the more important these activities become for our emotional and mental health, the more resistance we feel when it comes to doing them. It's important to fight for your health by recognizing this resistance and moving through it. Doing something is better than nothing. Each activity will help you build momentum in the right direction.

Books

I recommend reading quality books on Cognitive Therapy. Some of my favorite mental health books are not Christian, and so I take my faith and God's truth into each book with me. I ignore any proclaimed secular worldviews and only grab the helpful aspects for mental health. Make sure you are grounded in God's Word when you add secular mental health books.

> *To imagine none can teach you but those who are themselves saved from sin, is a very great dangerous mistake (John Wesley).*

In fact, within *Feeling Good*, I learned about bibliotherapy. This is learning and getting therapy by just reading quality, self-help books. This was fascinating to me and gave me a word for what I have been doing my whole life in a multitude of areas. Anytime I dive into a book on a particular subject, I am receiving quality instruction at little to no cost. This can span from anxiety, to finances, to computers, applications, history, etc. We don't need to go to school or a professional to learn something. The Internet, of course, took this to a new level with specific apps that bring libraries to our phone. Make sure you are taking advantage of the opportunities. And if you are getting professional therapy, be sure to supplement with bibliotherapy on your own. Always start with the Bible first and consider *Feeling Good* next.

Another book I recommend is *Finding Quiet* by J.P. Moreland. He wrote, "Gaining victory over anxiety includes cultivating the ability of noticing: being aware of the different feelings/sensations and their locations in the embodied soul."

I love Moreland's honesty that going to church once a week, reading the Bible each day, reading spiritual or psychological books, listening to worship music, etc., will likely not be enough for us anxiety to leave those who have severe anxiety and depression. Moreland's book is meat that you'll need to chew on, but it will be worth it.

Ten Ways to Know You Need to Go Back on Medication

Medications can be helpful for some individuals—even lifesaving (Burns, Feeling Good).

There may be a point you have to be honest with yourself and say, "I am not doing well. I need to reevaluate where I stand with my mental health." Below are ten ways that I know that I am struggling and need to go back on my medication or increase it. Your ten ways may look different.

1. Family says you are hard to live with.
2. You are found crying in your closet.
3. You find the people you really like to be super annoying.
4. You have no interest in doing anything fun.
5. You think you have to work endlessly.
6. People you love can't do anything right.
7. You can't do anything right.
8. You catastrophize to an irrational point.
9. You see nothing positive.
10. You are miserable and know there is something that can help.

Always Do What You Can

Samuel Johnson did not have the opportunity to live during a time when God had allowed for advances in medicine to help the genetic predisposition toward anxiety. So, he had to do what was within his power and ability. He wrote, "Every consideration by which groundless terrors may be removed adds something to human happiness."

Therefore, be mindful of what is in your control: you can read, learn, study, apply, and do your best to improve what is in your circle of control every day. Johnson read whatever he could in order to apply it to his life. Hallowell wrote, "He tore into literature, philosophy, theology, history, science, books about food and drink and games—everything. He searched for help far and wise" (*Worry*).

Johnson also worked hard and put exhaustive effort into each activity. He was a proponent of being honest about where you are. This is why I included "Ten Ways to Know You Need to Go Back on Meds." In fact, I credit God and the reading of the chapter on Samuel Johnson in Hallowell's book, *Worry*, for showing me that it was time to allow medication to help me again. Had Johnson had the help available to me today, he may have been able to go on and make even more amazing contributions to our world instead of taking his own life. I am no genius like Johnson, but God has gifted me with certain talents and treasures. By denying the help available to me, I was denying the opportunity for God to use me.

Johnson's story reminds me that I am experiencing something that is simply a part of our fallen world. It is not anything unique to me, but God can use it uniquely in His perfect way. Never forget that, friend.

~ Chapter 5 ~
# Daily Living

Dear Anxious Christian,

How are your mornings? Do you fly out of bed with an alarm? Toss and turn hoping you will fall back to sleep? Think about everything you need to do and spend 15 minutes dreading it all? Is prayer mixed into all the emotions? Is gratitude in your heart but fails to get into your head and body?

Mornings are my most difficult time of day. Everything negative always feels magnified in the morning. My worries, pain, to-do list, etc. What's ironic is that my favorite thing to do in the day is also in the morning: God-time.

Over the years I have learned how to work through this difficult time of the day. Have you evaluated the good mornings you have had to see what worked? It's important to monitor yourself: best times of day for work, difficult times of day for thoughts, necessary times for rest. Study yourself and ask God to show you how to better care for yourself.

It's so easy to get through the whole day and then to get to the end only to think that you got nothing done. Yet you know you got tons done. Perhaps you're worried it wasn't enough or the right things. Maybe you're anxious because you forgot what you need to be anxious about. For people who don't struggle with an anxiety disorder, the concept of forgetting what you are supposed to be worrying about is absurd. Worry and anxiety is our indication that we need to go to God and lift our cares to Him. It is the stimulus for required action: going to God.

Learning to let go and trust God is going to take a lot more effort for someone with an anxiety disorder. It's not going to look the way others think it should look. But 'others' can't see into the heart. They can't see the struggle of giving God the ball of your worry only to see it somehow right back in your hands. The obsessiveness of anxiety is irritating. But you're not alone. Not only are there others who understand, God understands. And only He matters, and He is not going anywhere.

> *No one will be able to stand against you all the days of your life. As I was with Moses, so I will be with you; I will never leave you nor forsake you (Joshua 1:5).*

Keep throwing Him your ball of anxiety—full of thoughts, concerns, and fears. Keep filling your mind with His Word and His love. Your prayers do not fall on deaf ears.

> *Therefore confess your sins to each other and pray for each other so that you may be healed. The prayer of a righteous person is powerful and effective (James 5:16).*

And although it may seem like your time with God is not improving your anxiety, continue anyway because His Word and love is powerful. It was during my time with God that He made me see that medicine is a gift He has given to us in this fallen world. Bottom line: don't quit.

Be completely humble and gentle; be patient, bearing with one another in love (Ephesians 4:2).

Spend a week studying Psalm 139. Dig into the truth of how God created you, the truth that God knows you, the truth that God protects you, the truth that you can ask Him to search your heart. Want to take it one step further? Memorize parts of it. Use the ideas in this book and the promptings of God's Spirit within you to come up with effective strategies to help with the mornings. And, remember, God's grace is new every day.

You have searched me, Lord, and you know me. You know when I sit and when I rise; you perceive my thoughts from afar (Psalm 139:1-2).

Decision-Making

Above all, my brothers and sisters, do not swear—not by heaven or by earth or by anything else. All you need to say is a simple "Yes" or "No." Otherwise you will be condemned (James 5:12).

Decision-making is one of my biggest areas of struggle in my anxiety. There is much double-mindedness that comes with my days because I am also a people-pleaser. The only time my choice is clear and precise is if I feel something is unfair or it touches a deeply held conviction. Anxiety about decisions yet to be made, and those that are complete, can lead to so much mental anguish. Besides people-pleasing, fear of making the wrong decision can also hinder me from taking action.

If you find that self-doubt haunts you and you're worried your decisions are wrong, then having a methodology for making decisions may help. For example, start with prayer.

Remember, if you make a wrong decision, your heavenly Father will forgive you and help you make things right—and even work it for your good.

And we know that in all things God works for the good of those who love Him, who have been called according to his purpose (Romans 8:28).

Next, make sure you are in God's Word regularly. Get a quality study Bible that is also full of insight and guidance to assist with understanding. I have two study Bibles that I use consistently for all my reading and study. Find one that works for you! Hearing God's direction often starts with His Word.

Then, if need be, seek counsel from a trusted Christian friend. (Read the first letter of John, which is entirely a response to *The Elect Lady* asking for godly counsel.) After I talk to God, I sometimes take the decisions I am struggling with to my husband and then another dear friend in Christ after. They help me to evaluate the concerns and the decisions. The goal is to make a decision and not look back. Unfortunately, I know that my decision-making process is usually long, tedious, and can be a waste of mental energy. When I don't follow a decision-making plan, it steals a great amount of my peace.

Let the peace of Christ rule in your hearts, since as members of one body you were called to peace. And be thankful (Colossians 3:15).

Peace in our hearts is a good indicator (like an umpire) of the right steps to take. God wants to be led by peace, not fear or people pleasing.

Jesus said, "Do not let your hearts be troubled. You believe in God; believe also in me" (John 14:1).

Habits

Another way to help with decision-making is to have quality habits in place. Habits (or routine) reduce the stress and mental fatigue in our schedules and activities so that we can thrive. The things we repeat are often what makes up a lot of our identity. Going to church regularly doesn't make one a Christian, but it makes up an important part of the Christian life. Take a look at what you repeat, and you will see where a great deal of your priorities are located.

This works in the positive and the negative. If you think worrying about a problem over and over again is going to solve it, you have made a habit of your worrying. J.P. Moreland wrote, "In some ways, anxiety is a learned habit that... forms grooves in the brain, heart muscle, and nervous system that trigger uncontrollable anxiety."

But if you make new habits and develop spiritual disciplines to lift worry such as prayer, journaling, or connecting with a trusted friend, you create a new pattern and eventually a new habit. Consider picking up books by Dr. Caroline Leaf who writes and teaches on neural plasticity and creating new neural pathways—essentially, performing "brain surgery" on yourself.

Obviously, worrying more about our anxiety is not going to help; therefore, a big part of dealing with anxiety is creating new habits in response to personal triggers. Habits are best when they are defined and specific. Noting the hardest times of your day and developing habits to counter those times can help tremendously.

For example, since I struggle with mornings, creating habits that happen early in the day, especially if there is accountability (someone waiting for me), helps to get me moving. I don't have time to think about whether I want to do it or not. The decision is set.

Time With God

The entire Word of God is a constant exhortation to believers to stop worrying (Ray Stedman).

One of the most important things you can do each day is spend time with God. He wants to hear from you. He wants you to cast your cares, concerns, and anxieties to Him. It is better to talk to God about them first than to talk to others and think about them ad nauseam.

Cast all your anxiety on Him because He cares for you (1 Peter 5:7).

Cast your cares on the Lord and He will sustain you; He will never let the righteous be shaken (Psalm 55:22).

God wants to help you. Comfort you. Guide you. But it's important to find time for Him. My God-time habit has been an important part of my life. I am not perfect or legalistic about it, but I can tell when I get lazy and don't make it a priority. I feel a lack of focus in my overall day. My God-time is usually in the morning at a local restaurant, coffee shop, or library (now that my kids are older). Ironically, I found my time with God more consistent when my kids were younger because kids force you into a schedule: waking, eating, playing. Now I feel tempted to work first, scroll social media, or get errands done.

God-time doesn't have to be monotonous or boring. Far from it. My God-time usually looks like this:
- Get Coffee.
- Journal (below I discuss my method of journaling).
- Read a chapter or two of the Bible (maybe not even that much) and take notes on it.
- Read and take notes on another book on a topic that I am diving into.

My God-time can last 20 minutes or an hour. The time and specifics are not important. It is the time you are spending with your heavenly Father that matters. He wants you to spend time with Him. He is not there only for our life's emergencies. He is our life.

Jesus said, "Come to me, all you who are weary and burdened, and I will give you rest" (Matthew 11:28).

One of my favorite parts of my God-time is journaling. Utilizing suggestions from books I have read throughout the years, I created and developed a method that has worked well for me:

1) Gratitude—List all the things that come to your mind that you are thankful to God for at that moment.
2) Confess—List the known sins in your life at that moment and your temptations.
3) WhooHoo—List the actions you have completed and the tasks you have accomplished.
4) Ugh—List the areas you have been procrastinating in or the actions that you failed to follow through on.
5) Revelation—Talk to God about what He has revealed to you recently and what it means to you.

6) Prayer—Bring God your cares, concerns, and requests.

A wonderful habit that Chuck Swindoll recommends is reading the book of Proverbs twice a year: January and July. Each of those months have 31 days, Proverbs has 31 chapters, and the months are exactly 6 months apart. He recommends applying the principles God reveals and observe the outcome, as well as reading the proverbs prayerfully. Swindoll also has an amazing book out called *Living the Proverbs* that is worth picking up and reading at least once, if not more.

Relaxing

Relaxation looks different for everyone. For me, I enjoy quiet time alone doing something I enjoy versus getting together with a large group of people. Don't feel bad if your type of relaxation is different than others. For example, before going to bed I like to study French. Other people would probably find that the opposite of relaxation. My husband enjoys going to a brewery and having a beer. I have learned to love that as well because it is how I can date him. He also doesn't mind if we play cards the entire time or if I bring work to do once in a while because he understands that doing nothing is not relaxing to me.

Be mindful if you struggle to relax at all or if you feel guilty doing it. I can feel bad taking time for myself. I battle the thought that I am more valuable when I am doing things. Our value is in who we are (children of God) not what we do. But this is very hard for certain personality types.

For those with an anxiety disorder, it can be freeing to be in cognitive activity as much as possible because you cannot have two thoughts at the same time. I cannot worry and work at the same time. I say cognitive activity because I can clean and still worry. I can wash dishes and not shut off my mind. This is why I enjoy studying to relax, because it forces my thoughts into that activity. I cannot learn French and have anxiety about tomorrow.

However, I won't throw myself into work so I don't have to deal with issues. I always need to deal with issues right away. But work, or even fun that requires cognitive activity (like my God-time), frees me from letting anxiety consume me. It's a balance that each person needs to find on their own.

You will keep in perfect peace those whose minds are steadfast, because they trust in you (Isaiah 26:3).

Physical Health

We have already talked briefly about thoughts, habits, relaxation, and decision making. However, I believe a key to maintaining my mental health is monitoring my physical health. This includes:
- Setting up routines for multiple areas of my life.
- Keeping an eye on my weight.
- Getting yearly labs done.
- Exercising regularly (an exercise I enjoy).
- Monitoring and logging my heart rate, steps, standing minutes, move minutes, etc.
- Moderation of alcohol, fried food, and sugar.

Being sick exponentially increases anxiety and negative thoughts. Doing your best to be as active as possible will help to manage your anxiety and improve your chances of longer life with less inflammation and disease. Motion is lotion!

Avoid Extremes

> *Life is a perpetual struggle to maintain balance between various opposing forces (Chuck Swindoll).*

We've talked about relaxing and our health, but the key is keeping balanced and avoiding extremes. Are you working *and* playing? I like the idea of remembering what you loved to do as a child and choosing to do it now as an adult. I think that is why coloring for adults became so popular. Take the areas that are extreme in your life and find a way to balance them.

> ***Be alert and of sober mind. Your enemy the devil prowls around like a roaring lion looking for someone to devour (1 Peter 5:8).***

My testimony is an example of how quickly ideas, passion, potential, and entrepreneurship can lead to being out of balance. My husband was there the whole time, but didn't have anywhere near the same number of negative consequences. He is just not created like I am. He does not suffer from the same problems. In fact, he states he has only had two major anxious moments in his entire life! I can't even relate to that. That is one reason I was so drawn to him, as well as being drawn to other non-anxious people. Both of my best friends are understanding of my anxiety, but can't relate to it at all. I love their stability. They are a critical part of helping me be aware of imbalances, extremism, and areas of concern in my life.

Money

Getting your finances under control is going to help relieve a lot of anxiety. Here are five recommended resources:

- Crown Ministries.
- Dave Ramsey.
- Focus on the Family.
- Quality financial podcasts and videos.
- Kiplinger's magazine.

Here are things I have done that have helped ease my anxiety in regards to finances:
- Completed Crown Financial Study and read Crown resources.
- Established a budget.
- Have an emergency fund.
- Save 3-6 months of salary.
- Save for retirement and choose low-cost mutual funds in all retirement accounts.
- Have some cash at all times at home.
- Track all income and expenses to see where I am wasting money.
- Have a will.
- Make spouse beneficiary to all accounts that are not joint and setup contingents to children.
- Save for all purchases and pay cash.
- Try to never pay interest.

Clear Clutter

There are quite a few different types of clutter and it can impact our anxiety level; it can be a trigger. John Maxwell organizes clutter into four types:
- Emotional (unforgiveness, bitterness, offense).
- Administrative (lack of organization).
- Calendar (poor time management, not removing time wasters).

- Trivial (important info you don't have to memorize and fail to write down).

Here are some ways to recognize your clutter triggers that lead to anxiety:
- How do you feel when you see your dining room or kitchen table packed with items?
- What's your first thought when you walk into your closet?
- How long does it take you to find important tax records or receipts?
- How many minutes a week do you spend trying to find items you lost?
- When you want to work on a project, do you feel you have nothing in place, or missing necessary items, and end up not doing anything?

Here are some suggestions to help clear your clutter and reduce unnecessary anxiety:
- Keep a basket at the entrance of your home or desk, and throw your keys in it when you get there.
- Have a password book and a password scheme (only changing the last few letters for different sites).
- Keep flat spaces as clean as possible and notice if it reduces your anxiety.
- Have a set place for certain projects and hobbies. Pre-set all the items you need for each project in one location.
- Organize all your receipts and taxes by year.
- Keep important documents used often on the cloud so you don't lose them.
- Backup your computer/files.

- Write down all your car maintenance so you don't have to guess when you need to get an oil change or do a tire rotation.
- Track all your time for a week and see where you are wasting it.
- Set time limits for social media sites on your phone.
- Join a recovery group where you can discuss the issues you have with relationships in your life or past.

Have a Schedule or a Priority List

I am self-employed and also homeschooling mom. Since I don't have a traditional day, I can have trouble with scheduling. In fact, most of the time I feel like I am always failing at one role when I concentrate on another. I feel like a bad mom when I am doing business. I feel like a bad wife if I am behind with work and can't get things done around the house. And I always feel bad when I take time out for my own mental and physical health.

Having a priority list or a realistic set of goals for a day or week helps me to keep my anxiety down. I usually put too much on my list and expect more out of myself than is possible. It reminds me of vacation, when I always take too much stuff to do, read, and enjoy on my time away. I usually end of up doing very little of it because it is unrealistic.

If you have anxiety at work (inside or outside the home) due to your schedule, take small steps to start putting your work life into a correct and realistic mindset. Be kind to your work self!

Work

Where do you work or study best? When are you able to get into flow—when you are fully engaged in the work you are doing? Since I am a business owner, and a stay at home mom, most of my work is done at home. However, I rarely get in a good work flow there. I prefer coffee shops, libraries, and parks. I enjoy listening to music (without words) to keep from getting distracted.

It's important to know where and when you thrive in the work God has put on your heart to do. When my kids were little, I had to ask for help or put them in activities that allowed me that free time. Make sure you are taking time to be the healthiest you that you can be. It may be necessary to find alone time at home when help is not available.

Honestly, when the kids were little, I got a lot of work and study done while they watched their favorite shows. We have all heard the statement, "Don't let the TV babysit your children," but I was so thankful that they sat and didn't move to give me the alone time I needed. Those shows, and later games, were more beneficial to the health of our family than any amount of negative they may have caused.

Christians who battle anxiety must study themselves and be creative to plan for calm and peaceful moments—even on vacations. My family is fully aware that when we are on vacation, I am going to have to take some time to rest mentally and, occasionally, physically. We cannot be good at whatever God has given us to do if we are not taking care of ourselves first.

Be still, and know that I am God; I will be exalted among the nations, I will be exalted in the earth (Psalm 46:10).

Bottom Line

The quality of your daily life will directly correlate with the amount of discipline you develop, grow, and apply. As Christ followers, we have the fruit of self-control. Some have more than others, so we must evaluate and ask God for an increase in this area as we do our part be mindful of being more disciplined each day.

For the Spirit God gave us does not make us timid, but gives us power, love and self-discipline (2 Timothy 1:7).

Remember how the Lord your God led you all the way in the wilderness these forty years, to humble and test you in order to know what was in your heart, whether or not you would keep his commands (Deuteronomy 8:2).

There are some important truths to remember when living and planning our days:
- God is allowing and using everything in our lives to build our character and accomplish His purpose.
- We are stewards of everything He has given us.
- Everything we have in this world is temporary.
- We need to use everything we have for God's Kingdom because we are accountable to Him.
- We can thank God for everything.

Take time to evaluate if you are using your work, influence, name, possessions and life to live the best life you can for Him. Anxiety disorders are not a disqualification! Our hearts are what matter to our Father.

You will never go wrong if you having the wisdom to know God, to study His ways, to discover his plan for your life, and let your relationship be your guide in everything.

Therefore this joy of mine has been made full. He must increase, but I must decrease (John 3:29b-30).

~ Chapter 6 ~
Have a Talk with Yourself

Dear Anxious Christian,

Step into my thoughts for a moment. Perhaps they will be of assistance and will show how something small can be the start of a bigger problem.

- **Me:** I suddenly feel so sad. Tears are on the edge.
- **Inner Me:** Why?
- **Me:** I don't know.
- **Inner Me:** Well, that's dumb. Figure it out or you'll be in this rut all day.
- **Me:** But I don't know why it has hit me so suddenly.
- **Inner Me:** Back track your thoughts. What is the last thing you remember thinking before being sad?
- **Me:** My to-do list. I have so much to get done that I don't know where to start. I need a notebook to write the list down, so I went looking for one I had stored somewhere.
- **Inner Me:** Did you find the notebook?
- **Me:** No.
- **Inner Me:** Did the depression kick in when you were thinking about making a list or when you were looking for the notebook?
- **Me:** When I was looking for it.
- **Inner Me:** So then maybe the fact that you have multiple areas that lack the organization you need triggered the sadness.

- **Me:** Maybe.
- **Inner Me:** OK. You're going to pray about where it is and wait for revelation. While you're waiting, go do something else. Laundry. Cleaning. Anything.

Do you know the triggers for your anxiety? Have you tried to backtrack your thoughts just like you backtrack your steps when you have lost something? Try it.

Negativity

Anyone who knows me well will tell you that I have a serious bent toward negativity. In fact, I asked my husband and closest friends to give me a negativity to positivity ratio. It ended up being 70:30. I gave myself a ratio of 65:35, so I wasn't far off or in any kind of denial. I know that I am very negative and my creativity doesn't help at all. It is amazing how creatively negative I can be.

One very important part of my being on medication is the obvious increase in positivity (or less negativity). Off medication, I can only see problems in the most beautiful of situations. I see the thorns of the roses, and never the roses themselves. On medication, I am far more aware of the good around me. I believe this is another clear indication that my anxiety is a disorder. Therefore, my negativity baseline does fluctuate depending on whether or not I am on medication. (I share this chart in Chapter 2.) However, it does always lean more negative than positive.

There are many downsides of negativity, but one is the obvious increased anxiety it causes. One of the projects I am working on is getting my negativity from 70:30 to 49:51 in three years. I call it my positivity project. I am fully aware that the goal to be positive a greater amount of time than negative is going to take a mighty work of God within me. I know I can't do it on my own. But I do have a vision, and I think that is the first step.

Where there is no revelation, people cast off restraint; but blessed is the one who heeds wisdom's instruction (Proverbs 29:18).

My goal to be more positive than negative in three years may seem too extreme or even impossible. It's trying to change at such a deep level that some may think I am setting myself up for failure. However, it doesn't cost anything to believe or to try. And if I fail, I have a chance of being a little less negative and a little more positive. It's a win/win challenge and vision. I lose nothing by putting my faith in God's power within me.

What is your negative to positive ratio? If you asked others, would you be close to their numbers? You may have been born automatically with a more positive, relaxed attitude. Celebrate that. But if you were not, make an effort to take bite-size bites of positivity in your day.

This positivity could also be approached from a happiness perspective. If I am happier, would I be more positive? Sonja Lyubomirsky, in her book *The How of Happiness,* states that 50% of our happiness is already set by our genes and so some people are happier more naturally than others. She states that only 10% of our happenings is due to our circumstances and 40% is within our control and based on our choices. It is this 40% that I am working on with my positivity project. This percentage should give us hope of improvement and, I believe, is exponentially increased when partnering this hope with God in the endeavor.

Self-Worth

Many of our feelings result from our thoughts about ourselves. How is your self-esteem? Your self-compassion? Is it based on achievements or is it based on who you are in Christ?

Being that I did not know Christ until I was 24, and that I was raised in a home where I was not taught about God in any way and everything worth of any value was achieved, I have hard time not attaching my worth with action. In addition, the actions I did take were not often good enough for my mother and that created a lot of perfectionism in my life.

Taking time to evaluate what you say about yourself is important as our self-talk results in changes in our thoughts and feelings. When our self-talk is negative, it makes us feel worse which then leads to more negative self-talk and more depression. It is a cycle.

> *During periods of depression, you lose some of your capacity for clear thinking; you have trouble putting things in to proper perspective (Burns,* Feeling Good*).*

Perhaps you have a similar block toward loving and being positive toward yourself, yet you are able to be loving toward another who may be feeling the same way. Maybe you wonder why you can't have that same conversation with yourself. I believe it may be an indicator of doubt when it comes to accepting God's love for yourself. After all, you know everything about you and you wonder if God can really love *all of you.*

As Christians, we know that God loves everyone the same. We know that He can't love us more or less than He does right now. But we have trouble believing it and accepting it. What if you talked to yourself as you would your best friend in the same situation? Or, even better, have a conversation with God in writing. I think you'll be surprised how it will help you break that negative self-talk habit.

Here is an actual (written) conversational prayer I had with God about my anxiety:

Father, I feel like a failure that I can't get off my meds and function well emotionally.

Child, you were doing so well on the medication, but you let yourself be guilted into thinking you needed to get off. And you did that on your own. I did not tell you to get off of it.

True. There's a new Christian book I am reading it and it says I can be mentally healthy without them if I just think right. I want to please you, and I don't think I am pleasing you when I am on this medication.

You please me based on who you are, not what medications you do or don't take. You come to Me, and I'll guide you. The medication is a tool I have given you in this life to help you. I am the One Who allows it to work.

I am thankful for it, Father. Without it, I don't feel I am the best me I want to be. With it, I am closer. But what about long-term?

I want you to have life until it overflows. What overflows in your life when you are on this medication (and not stressing about being on it)? When are you living life in abundance? Off or on medication?

Oh, Father, on this small amount of medication I am loving life more. Joy and peace are easier, more accessible.

You have wasted hours this week in sickness from going off your meds and worrying about being on it. Let it go. Stay on it and live with Me each day. You cannot put Me first, or

be helpful to others, when you are consumed with what is happening in your head.

I am so sorry.

No need to be sorry. Let's just press on!

Thank you for Your help, Father!

You're welcome. Are you ready to go back to living each day and working on the things you can control?

Yes, Lord.

Good. I love you.

Kristen Neff, an expert on self-compassion writes about her revelation concerning the difference between self-esteem and self-compassion:

> *I realized that self-compassion was the perfect alternative to the relentless pursuit of self-esteem. Why? Because it offers the same protection against harsh self-criticism as self-esteem, but without the need to see ourselves as perfect or as better than others. In other words, self-compassion provides the same benefits as high self-esteem without its drawbacks (Neff, Self-Compassion).*

Learning self-compassion helps us be "more resilient and better able to regain emotional well-being after adversity and less prone to anxiety and depression" (Moreland).

Moreland provides practical steps for increasing our self-compassion in his book *Finding Quiet*:
- Take moments to remind yourself that the time has come to stop being so hard on yourself and stop beating yourself up.

- When you fail, put yourself in a dear friend's shoes and ask how you would respond to them if they had done the same thing (I am very bad at this, which is why I do the previously mentioned writing method).
- Practice a gentle attitude toward yourself.

I highly recommend reading all of J.P. Moreland's books. They can be challenging reads, but they are worth the time and effort.

Peace Stealers

Five enemies of peace inhabit within us - avarice, ambition, envy, anger, and pride; if these were to be banished, we should infallibly enjoy perpetual peace (The Italian Poet Petrarch).

Being negative is definitely a stealer of our peace. Some others, as Petrarch states, include extreme desire for wealth (avarice), jealousy (comparing), anger (which I dedicate a later chapter to), pride, and…passion/ambition. We are told that passion is important and instrumental to our success and purpose, but when it is out of balance or outside of God's Will, it can be a peace stealer and an anxiety booster. Our passion needs reflection, as does the more obvious peace stealers.

I am a very ambitious and passionate person. I have the gifts of leading and teaching, and I can't sit still long doing only one thing. I have many projects going at the same time, and I keep lists of ideas so I don't forget. I always hope to use my time, talent, and treasure for God's glory. All this can lead to increased anxiety because it steals my peace. The truth is, I usually have too much going on and yet am still disgruntled that I am not making more of an impact. I rarely see the impact I am actually making in my circle of influence because it is not as grandiose as the impact I want to make (ambition/passion).

A heart at peace gives life to the body, but envy rots the bones (Proverbs 14:30).

There is probably an innumerable amount of peace stealers in our lives that are contributing to our anxiety when we consider that each of us is different and our battle with anxiety is very specific and unique. This is where taking the time to talk to God about it is important so that He can show us any areas we have not thought about or are blind to. Our peace stealers will not always be so obvious: like unforgiveness, which we will discuss in the chapter on anger.

Where there is strife, there is pride, but wisdom is found in those who take advice (Proverbs 13:10).

One of the hard truths God pointed out to me was that my desire to be right and inform people of their wrongness was causing me less peace in my life. For example, if you read my testimony already, you know that the things that I have heard pastors say on the pulpit have absolutely crushed and angered me. Some of these pastors are local and well known to me. One time I did try and bring up my concern about what was being said, but the conversation ended with more frustration on my end.

We can't switch churches every time we hear something we don't like, unless the concerns are based on biblical doctrine. Then moving is necessary. However, when we don't agree on non-doctrinal comments, we need to decide how to handle it with the most peace. For me, since I don't feel comfortable talking with these pastors about their comments, I have decided to pray for people within their circle of control to speak into their hearts. It's not my job to change them. It's God's. Do you have any peace stealers in your life when it comes to wanting to be right?

> *Peace I leave with you; my peace I give you. I do not give to you as the world gives. Do not let your hearts be troubled and do not be afraid (John 14:27).*

Confessions

What we say to ourselves matters. My negativity, constant battle with anxiety, and strengths that can quickly become weaknesses lead me to say useless things to myself. Coming up with confessions that you can read over and over again helps. Here are some examples:
- I love myself and that includes everything I see wrong with myself.
- I give myself permission to be imperfect.
- I approve of myself, even in my imperfect state.
- I can enter God's rest.
- Every flaw is something God can use for His purpose.
- God strengthens me in my weaknesses.
- My weaknesses help me lean on God constantly.
- I know God sees my heart and knows it completely.
- My self-worth is not based on what others think of me.
- God doesn't want me confused, defeated, or not living in peace.
- God loves my desire to be the best I can be.
- God is guiding me and making my paths straight.
- God is opening the right doors at the right times for me.

- I do not struggle trying to make things happen according to my own desires and timeframe.
- I live in grace and not in works.
- I am right with God because of my faith, not my works.
- God's love is a free gift; I cannot earn it or change it.
- God's love for me is unconditional, I cannot earn it.
- I will prosper when I follow God's ways, not my own ways.
- I seek God's approval, not the approval of man.
- I guard my heart, know my destination, and keep my attention focused on God's will for my life.
- I am fulfilling my destiny through my trials.
- I evaluate my life via God's Word and aim to remove any distractions.
- I protect my mind and will not settle for less than God's best.

Useful Thinking

Along with confessions, it is important to try and change the way we think (hence my positivity project). But changing our thinking from anxious to useful/positive, can look different for us all. Maybe telling yourself to knock it off helps. Maybe deliberately doing a positive action each day will help. The possibilities are endless. I also like sitting and imagining Jesus talking right to me about what is going on. He says hard things I need to hear in love. Sometimes I need to say hard things to myself. I find it is best when I write them out. For example, here is a letter I wrote to myself a few years ago:

Dear Lilly,
I know you are struggling with things right now: chronic pain, stomach issues, guilt, depression, and

not understanding why you feel certain ways and think the way you do. But you know God has you. You know in your heart that you love Him and He loves you. It's easy to get consumed with research and fear. How about we find a verse you can think about when this lack of understanding wants to take your focus?

The problem is that we have been thinking the wrong way for so many years and have never learned how to think in such a way that it is not continually and consistently putting us into a state of useless thinking which feeds our anxiety and makes it worse. Changing our patterns of thinking is going to require work and awareness. Thankfully, God has given us many resources and it is amazing how much of the secular help in the world is clearly shown in God's Word. For example, when we take our thoughts captive (2 Corinthians 10:5) we are engaging in what physiologists call Cognitive Behavioral Therapy.

Cognitive Behavioral Therapy (CBT)

The worrier habitually misinterprets the data of everyday life in such a way that his thoughts run in a fearful direction (Hallowell, Worry).

CBT has been very helpful in altering my self-talk. Since I take suggestions, guidance, and comments as offense and criticism, I need ways to be sure I am interpreting events in my life properly with the right perspective. My favorite book on CBT is *Feeling Good* by Dr. David Burns. He wrote:

Your feelings result from the message you give yourself. In fact, your thoughts often have much more to do with how you feel than what is actually happening in your life.

CBT is all about retraining our brain to change and abolish negative thought patterns. It can be "at least as effective as drugs" for some people (Burns, *Feeling Good*). It's about taking the situations or comments in our lives and head and being realistic about them. It helps change our self-talk, which for many is distorted and leans toward the negative and results in anxiety and depression.

I usually bounce a lot of my self-talk off my husband who can give me a more realistic view since I am very hard on myself. The irony is that I can have great moments of encouraging and supportive self-talk, but it is not automatic and takes a lot of effort. I wish it was automatic, but wishing never changed anything. I ask God to help me to apply what I learn and medication gives me the balance I need to do it.

Alter your "State"

Maybe the best way to change your thinking is to change your "state." This can take the form of turning on music, dancing, various activities (like cooking, cleaning, etc.), exercise, sex, or doing something special for someone else.

I know that when I am anxious or depressed, I have no desire to socialize. Yet, any type of environment that leads me to laugh is helpful. Sharing and listening to others is also advantageous (which is why I recommend Celebrate Recovery so much). It's the work up to these altered "states" that is so difficult. Some may prefer to lay on the couch and binge watch TV and others, like me, will work myself to the point of exhaustion before doing those necessary "state" changes like exercise or socializing.

Steps to Work Through

Anderson and Miller give 10 helpful steps (below) to overcoming anxiety in *Freedom from Fear*—a book I highly recommend you read. Remember, overcoming anxiety is different than getting rid of it; it's doing what is in your power, putting it into a balanced perspective, and casting all of it to God.

1. Go to God in prayer.
2. Resolve all known personal spiritual conflicts.
3. State the problem.
4. Separate the facts from the assumptions.
5. Determine your active response (what you can control).
6. List everything related to the situation that is your responsibility.
7. Follow through on your list of responsibilities. Become accountable to someone for fulfilling your goals.
8. If you have fulfilled your responsibility and continue to walk with God in prayer, according to Philippians 4:6-8, the rest is God's responsibility.

~ Chapter 7 ~
Accepting the Less than Perfect Days

Dear Anxious Christian,

There may be days where you just can't seem to shake the anxious feelings you have. You've prayed, called your sponsor, talked to your spouse, exercised, read, etc., and nothing worked. You are still productive but you feel the constant heaviness of the anxiety over everything you do. There are brief moments of peace when you are fully engaged in something, but then it comes back. And, with it, brings disappointment and feelings of shame. What if, on those days, we recognize that it's just *one of those days* and stop fighting it.

When we have done all that the situation requires, we should now rest in God's hands. Much easier said than done, and sometimes it requires engaging our minds in other activities. Maybe watch a movie, read a fiction novel, color, play some games; choose something fun. I have found that when I can't shake a feeling, it may be God's way of telling me to 'turn off' for a while and just enjoy some rest, peace, or fun. It's OK to have hard days; He still loves you. And we are probably so hard on ourselves most of the time that it may be the clue we need to allow ourselves to be less serious and re-hand it all over to Him. Again, and again.

My flesh and my heart may fail, but God is the strength of my heart and my portion forever (Psalm 73:26).

Depression

The Lord is close to the brokenhearted and saves those who are crushed in spirit (Psalm 34:18).

When depression piles on, it can feel difficult to think clearly. I know that I struggle with perspective. Every issue feels bigger than it actually is to someone who is not struggling with depression and anxiety. In fact, it is often a vicious circle. The more I think, the more depressed I feel, and, in turn, the more dramatically negative my thinking becomes.

Your negative thoughts, or cognitions, are the most frequently overlooked symptoms of your depression... Your emotions result entirely from the way you look at things. When you are depressed or anxious, your thoughts will always be illogical, distorted, unrealistic, or just plain wrong (Burns, Feeling Good*).*

As we discussed in the previous chapter, Cognitive Behavioral Therapy (CBT) is going to help with this vicious negative thought cycle. When we have an accurate understanding of what is going on in our lives, our thought patterns and emotions are going to be more stable. Burns' book helps understand that our thinking (mental tuning) can be adjusted and the result can clear out the distortion (depression).

One of the absolute best tools I learned from Burns' book was the ten cognitive distortions that he says are the basis for all depression. I also found the distortions to be very applicable to my anxiety and self-talk. *Feeling Good* goes into great detail about these distortions; therefore, I highly recommend you pick the book up to thoroughly understand them and enjoy the benefits of some quality bibliotherapy!

The Ten Cognitive Distortions
1. All-or-Nothing Thinking
2. Overgeneralization
3. Mental Filter
4. Disqualifying the Positive
5. Jumping to Conclusions
6. Magnification and Minimization
7. Emotional Reasoning
8. Should Statements
9. Labeling and Mislabeling
10. Personalization

Below, I have listed ten questions to ask yourself (grab your journal) about each cognitive distortion to help understand them more thoroughly.

1. Are you expecting to be perfect at everything?
2. Do you expect that something specific will happen just because that is what happened last time?
3. At the end of the day, do you dwell about the one negative thing that happened?
4. Are you good at taking the one positive in a situation and making it negative?
5. If someone looks at their watch while you are talking to them, do you assume they are bored?
6. Do you magnify what you do wrong and minimize what you do right?

7. If you feel bad, do you assume you must have done something to feel that way?
8. Do you try and get yourself motivated and moving by using should statements?
9. If you just sit and enjoy a movie, do you feel lazy?
10. Do you feel negative events are somehow your fault?

Spiritual Health Amidst Depression

As a follower of Christ, it is easy to assume that feelings of depression may be an indication of a lack of closeness to God. We may even attach the label of worthlessness to ourselves and then that thought makes the depression deepen. But these thoughts mistake our mental health with our spiritual health. C.S. Lewis said, "A man's spiritual health is exactly proportional to his love for God" (*Mere Christianity*). It does not say our mental health is proportional to it. Our struggle with neurological anxiety, or circumstantial anxiety, and the depression that often follows, is not to be assumed to be an indicator of some failure with our relationship with God.

> ***"For I know the plans I have for you," declares the Lord, "plans to prosper you and not to harm you, plans to give you hope and a future" (Jeremiah 29:11).***

Just as I can hug and cry on my earthly father's shoulder, so can I go to my Heavenly Father. God understands my hurts and does not send me away because of my pain. I can get depressed because I can't fix my anxiety disorder, but I know God is able to make things happen if He chooses to do so. He is in control of everything. When He doesn't, I need to assume that it is what is best for me and my purpose.

Trust in the Lord with all your heart and lean not on your own understanding; in all your ways submit to Him, and He will make your paths straight (Proverbs 3:5-6).

Pleasing God

When you get to the end of the day, or perhaps multiple times during the day, you may think that you have displeased God. You may think that you can't please Him at all. But it's important to remember what we need to do to please the Lord. It is not having a perfect day with checked off to-do lists, a clean house, respectful children, or whatever other perfectionist thought we may have in our heads. There is one thing we must do to please God: believe in Jesus.

Then they asked Him, "What must we do to do the works God requires?" Jesus answered, "The work of God is this: to believe in the one He has sent" (John 6:28-29).

When we truly believe in Jesus, we have acknowledged our sin, His sacrifice, His resurrection, and aim to follow and obey Him as our Lord and Leader. It is easy for me to forget this is in all my failures. Therefore, I re-read Rick Warren's *The Purpose Driven Life* to remind myself of how I please God.

The Lord is pleased with those who worship Him and trust in His love (Psalm 147:11).

Our Helper

The Spirit of Truth, Whom the world cannot receive, because it neither sees Him nor knows Him; but you know Him, for He dwells with you and will be in you (John 14:17).

Every day we are growing and changing because we have the Holy Spirit within us. This is so hard for the anxious Christian to remember, but things are harder if we try to do anything without leaning on and trusting God. Our successful walk in Christ in this world begins with believing in Him and the Holy Spirit becomes our "Helper." When we believe and follow Christ, everything else will fall in place as God has designed. It doesn't mean it will always be lollipops and roses, but we can trust that the Creator of the universe is at work and only asks for our belief.

Notice that the Holy Spirit is also called the "Spirit of Truth." He is working in us to bring us to new levels of awareness. This obviously includes awareness of our anxiety and mental health.

When we lean on God in all our problems, and that includes our bent toward anxiety, He will keep us stable. This stability is because we are relying on the strength of our mighty and firm foundation: Christ. When we do not let Satan work through our anxiety by letting us think that we are failures, and instead focus on our belief in Christ, we increase the likelihood of change in our thinking/behavior because we are instead focusing on the stable Rock of our faith and trusting His purposes.

When we put God first, He will always lift us up. Having anxiety is not an indicator that you are displeasing to God. It is also NOT an indicator that you are failing to put Him first.

Magnification

When we have days that are less than our idea of perfect, we need to take a look at what we are magnifying. When we magnify something, we enlarge it so much that it is all we see.

> *I will praise God's name in song and glorify Him with thanksgiving (Psalm 69:30).*

We need to make God bigger than our problems. I try and do this by going to Him about everything. Worship in the midst of anxious thoughts is also a great way to magnify God. I will admit, I struggle to sing when I am overly worried about something. I need to find other ways to worship and magnify Him such as journaling, listening to podcasts of my favorite Bible teachers, or just listening to worship music.

It's ok to be different from other people. What works for one may not work for another. The key is to find ways to magnify God in your situation and life.

> *And let us run with perseverance the race marked out for us, fixing our eyes on Jesus, the pioneer and perfecter of faith. For the joy set before Him, He endured the cross, scorning its shame, and sat down at the right hand of the throne of God (Hebrews 12:2).*

Worship doesn't have to look the same for everyone. As long as we our turning our attention from our anxious thoughts and putting them on God, then we are magnifying God more than the problem—even while we are talking about the problem with Him.

See, I am doing a new thing! Now it springs up; do you not perceive it? I am making a way in the wilderness and streams in the wasteland (Isaiah 43:19).

Disappointing Others

I am, more often than not, disappointing to myself in a multitude of different ways. It is an area I work on. But one of the hardest situations for me to handle is when I think or know that I am disappointing others: God, my husband, my friends. I know in my heart that God cannot love me anymore or any less than He always has. I believe I put most of this disappointment on myself. God forgives and forgets our sins (Hebrews 10:17), yet the struggle to forgive ourselves is extraordinary.

I asked my husband if I am disappointing him in any way at home, or if he has any expectations I'm not meeting. Of course, when you ask such a question, you need to be willing to hear the answer. We ended up having a long conversation about the topic, and he agreed that I put a lot of the "expectations" on myself.

Do everything without grumbling or arguing... (Philippians 2:14).

In a way, the fear of disappointing others is a complaint against myself. I am grumbling about how I am doing because it doesn't meet my own expectations. We know that complaining is a sin, so if God has not shown me an area that needs true correction, am I not just complaining and grumbling about myself instead of being grateful for who God as made me? Am I not focusing on what I don't have instead of being grateful for what I do have? How can God reward and grow me when I am not thankful for the little things?

> ***Rejoice always, pray continually, give thanks in all circumstances; for this is God's will for you in Christ Jesus (1 Thessalonians 5:16-19).***

Am I trying to achieve the things God has put on my heart, or am I trying to achieve my own ways while leaving a path of disappointment? God tells us not to seek our own way, but to seek Christ (Philippians 2:21). Evaluate who you fear to disappoint. It might be yourself.

Procrastination

One of the problems with anxiety, and then the resulting depression, is that it disables. It can stop us from moving. It can stop us from doing the things we want to do and the things we need to do. Burns calls it do-nothingism and explains it like this:

> *One of the most destructive aspects of depression is the way it paralyzes your willpower. In its mildest form you may simply procrastinate about doing a few odious chores. As your lack of motivation intensifies, virtually any activity appears so difficult that you become overwhelmed by the urge to do nothing. Because you accomplish very little, you feel worse and worse* (Feeling Good).

The irony is we act in ways that are not the best for us and then we get sad and repeat the behavior over and over again. We need to bring this procrastination over to God and also evaluate when it occurs? Is it when the events of life or triggers compile? Is there just one thing you can do to "alter your state" so you can take a small step out of that procrastination?

~ Chapter 8 ~
Relationships

Dear Anxious Christian,

There is amazing power in relationships. Obviously, our most important relationship is the one we have with Christ. Our anxiety can put a strain on many of our relationships, especially the one we have with ourselves. But our relationships help us get through the rough times and it's important we stay true and honest in them. Making time for self and others is vital in our mental health. Quality relationships can also help us take our mind off ourselves. When we come into relationship with Jesus, we get the Holy Spirit and His fruit.

But the fruit of the Spirit is love, joy, peace, patience, kindness, goodness, faithfulness, gentleness and self-control. Against such things there is no law (Galatians 5:22-23).

Therefore, peace is in us. It is part of the foundation of our relationship with God. That core peace is unaffected by circumstances because it is from God. Now, I have seen some amazing peace in believers and maybe that fruit is not given out in equal amounts. We only know that it is given. I pray for increased peace and other fruits of the Holy Spirit, and I believe God is answering my prayer in the way that He sees fit and on His timetable. I encourage you to pray for increased fruit in your relationship with God too.

Family

Relationships can cause so much anxiety in our lives. Unfortunately, we have no control over anyone else; all we can do is what is in our circle of control. Sometimes that means establishing boundaries. I had to establish boundaries with my own family in various ways. For example, my step-father was verbally abusive and his words hurt me for years. I eventually had to eliminate all contact with him, which made my relationship with my mother much harder. However, she was also very hurtful with her own words toward me, so that boundary with my step-father helped reduce the amount of interaction with her. Both hated everything I stood for, and my relationships with them caused a tremendous amount of anxiety in my life. But I always aimed to be the best daughter I could be within healthy boundaries.

> *Whatever you do, work at it with all your heart, as working for the Lord, not for human masters, since you know that you will receive an inheritance from the Lord as a reward. It is the Lord Christ you are serving (Colossians 3:23-24).*

I would love to say that everyone understood the anxiety in my life and were supportive of my decision to go on medication, but that would not be true. My father felt that anxiety and depression were mental toxins that I was allowing and giving action to. Others said I was weak. Since most of my family is not Christian, I did not get from them the "have more faith" comments. However, they were similar: I just needed to put more effort, time, and willpower into being less anxious.

I felt like a failure.

Do not let any unwholesome talk come out of your mouths, but only what is helpful for building others up according to their needs, that it may benefit those who listen (Ephesians 4:29).

It's important to have people in your life that understand your anxiety and can see the difference when you are on medication and when you are off. My husband is fully aware of the healing the medicine provides my mental health. Of course, so am I. Using guidelines that I mention in Chapter 4 —Ten Ways to Know You Need to Go Back on Medication—I evaluate how well my mental health is doing.

I asked my husband to write up a statement for this chapter to share his experience with living with someone with an anxiety disorder. I know it is hard living with me and my anxiety has taken a toll on our relationship through the years. I am grateful God gave me a patient, understanding husband who never gave up on me through all the struggles.

To put things in perspective, on a scale of 1-10, my typical "normal" day of anxiety hovers between zero and one. Anxiety and its counterpart, depression, seem to be constants in my wife's life. Over the twenty plus years of marriage, I have developed two strategies when these emotions occur in her.

If the issue at hand is very over the top ridiculous, I will make a light joke by saying, "And an asteroid could also land on our house." This cues her into the fact that she is worrying about nothing. We laugh and move on. When she has a more "realistic" worry/concern, then I pay attention to what she is saying and either agree with her that there is an actionable item there (like getting on the roof to check for wind damage after a storm) or it is something that we need to pay attention to more closely.

Since anxiety is very low for me, and I am a "go with the flow" type of person, I tend to not care about things unless they are very serious. This can be a detriment to my life in many different ways. I now see my wife's issues in a different light and utilize them to their fullest potential (protecting assets, saving money, protecting loved ones, personal health, etc.). By doing so, we make lemonade out of lemons and utilize her "weaknesses" for positive gain.

Friends

I am drawn to people who are not anxious. I am married to someone who would have to work just as hard to be anxious as I work to be peaceful. Anxiety is draining, for the person who feels it and the person who is around it. I understand that I am more of a high maintenance friend because of this aspect of my life. Surrounding ourselves with people who recognize their weaknesses and can empathize with our struggles goes a long way toward having healthy friendships. Find those people who are calm, be honest with them about your anxiety, and watch the relationship flourish.

Therefore encourage one another and build each other up (1 Thessalonians 5:11a).

Here is a statement from one of my best friends and our relationship considering my bent toward anxiety:

My best friend is the person I most often encounter who struggles through an anxiety disorder. I've learned a lot from our friendship. Things most people would find a minor inconvenience can quickly become so overwhelming that she cannot function. When this happens, I don't try and "talk her down." Generally, that won't work.

I've learned to let her talk through why something has suddenly pushed her buttons. Most of the time it is not the last thing that overwhelmed her—it was several minor things on top of other minor things that becomes too much to deal with. Letting her talk through everything often allows her to take a step back and see that it's not as bad as she thought. Sometimes she just needs a sounding board. Sometimes she just needs someone to help her get out of the rabbit hole she's gone down. All of the time, she needs a friend.

Hospitality

It is likely that you prefer to be alone and keep social engagements short and sweet. You may struggle with, or avoid, hospitality and hosting all together. You are not alone.

One of my most stressful situations is hosting family and friends, especially for overnight occasions. I want to entertain but not control. Yet I find that few guests speak their mind, and I am forced to figure out what they would like to do.

I find the easiest way to deal with this is to make plans and also give choices and ask them to rank their preference. Most guests don't want to be a burden, so they are trying to be as easy going as possible. Another approach is being straight up with your guests about your anxiety and how much it would help if they voiced their opinions so you don't have to guess.

Remember to take time for yourself during these events if they are longer than a day. You need quiet time with God to relieve the tension the events may be bringing into your life. It is easy to forgo the daily things that bring us moments of joy when we have guests for periods of time.

Circle of Control

Obviously, we can't control others. They are not within our circle of control. Unfortunately, it doesn't stop us from trying. I do label myself as a control freak. It was something that my environment created within me when I was young due to the divorce of my parents. I was the middle child and took it upon myself for decades to keep them separated. Weddings, funerals, graduations…I worked diligently to keep them apart because they didn't like one another. It was exhausting. Now, I have to put effort into not controlling every situation and what people are doing. And I don't do it well.

There are also those relationships that are toxic and need clear boundaries. As I mentioned, my step-father was verbally abusive toward me and it caused nothing but problems for years between my mother and myself. I eventually had to have no contact with him, as it was damaging my mental health. I could not stop him from being mean and hurtful, but I could control whether or not I was around him. For over ten years, when I visited my mother, we always met at a restaurant. I never went to her home once I established the boundary with her husband. It also helped reduce the amount of negativity I received from her, which was also quite significant.

Have you ever noticed how things with borders look nicer and cleaner? Our pictures have borders. Our floors and walls have boarders. The streets have border lines. Sidewalks are a type of boarder in a neighborhood. Borders in our home can give us a clean and peaceful feeling without even knowing it.

Borders in our life, and boundaries in our relationships, help keep our days healthy and beautiful. Take note of the areas within your control in your relationships. Establish and maintain relationships that bring you joy and peace. Fill your social calendar with people you love to hang out with and who bring out the best in you.

Do What You Can to Live in Peace

When there is tension at work or home, the days can drag and emotions can get out of control. A big part of keeping the anxiety out of your life is doing your best to keep the peace as much as it depends on you. This includes making amends whenever necessary and as soon as possible.

Part of the Christ-centered recovery program called Celebrate Recovery is making amends whenever possible. And when I don't want to make amends, the accountability group part of the program helps me to tackle those areas of struggle. In fact, studies show that when people regularly meet together to talk and discuss issues, there is more likely to be physical and mental healing—there is power in connectedness and strength in numbers (Hallowell).

The amount of peace I feel when I know I have done all I can to keep strife out of my life is priceless. Of course, just because I have done all I can do to maintain the peace, doesn't mean the other person will agree to do the same. But we can't change them. We can only control ourselves.

The goal is to do what we can to keep our side of the street clean. Some people are never going to like us and we're never going to please them. All we can do is our part. Keeping our side of the street clean means we apologize when we have done something we know is wrong. It means forgiving others whether they have apologized or not. We need to remember who the real enemy is in this world.

> *For our struggle is not against flesh and blood, but against the rulers, against the authorities, against the powers of this dark world and against the spiritual forces of evil in the heavenly realms (Ephesians 6:12).*

Ask God what relationships you need to address so that you can reduce your anxiety in those areas.

~ Chapter 9 ~
Positives of Anxiety?

Whatever struggle or setback you face is intended to empower and purify you (David Jeremiah).

Dear Anxious Christian,

One of the books I discovered while researching for this one was *The Anxiety Opportunity* by Curtis Chang. Although my anxiety has caused me numerous problems throughout my life, it has also provided me with opportunities for spiritual growth. Chang does a wonderful job of explaining anxiety in the Christian's life and the opportunities of what can come *through* it:

Anxiety is not an obstacle to spiritual maturity. It is not some moral flaw we must not get rid of in order to grow toward Jesus. Anxiety is also not irrelevant, as if our mental health is disconnected from our spiritual health. Anxiety can be the very place where we meet Jesus. Through anxiety we can actually become more like Him.

While we are waiting and praying for God's healing power in our anxiety, we can recognize the advantages of the bent toward anxiety—whether it is due to genetics, stress, or circumstances.

Advantages

- It humbles us:

  For our light and momentary troubles are achieving for us an eternal glory that far outweighs them all (2 Corinthians 4:17).

- It forces us to lean on God and draws us closer to Him:

  God will sometimes deliberately deny us human help in order that we may learn how much greater is the help waiting for us from the invisible kingdom (Ray Stedman).

  Pain is God's megaphone (C.S. Lewis).

  An awareness of an anxious spirit should drive us to find the peace of God by turning to Him and assuming our responsibility to think [true, honorable, right, pure, lovely...] thoughts (Anderson & Miller).

- It forces us to take faith breaks and disciplines us:

  Jesus went out as usual to the Mount of Olives, and His disciples followed Him. On reaching the place, He said to them, "Pray that you will not fall into temptation." He withdrew about a stone's throw beyond them, knelt down and prayed, "Father, if you are willing, take this cup from me; yet not my will, but yours be done." An angel from heaven appeared to Him and strengthened Him. And being in anguish, he prayed more earnestly, and his sweat was like drops of blood falling to the ground (Luke 22:39-44).

- It forces us to take heed of our thoughts:

    Can any one of you by worrying add a single hour to your life? (Matthew 6:27)

    Therefore do not worry about tomorrow, for tomorrow will worry about itself. Each day has enough trouble of its own (Matthew 6:34).

- It forces us to reevaluate our priorities:

    For where your treasure is, there your heart will be also (Matthew 6:21).

- It warns us of danger:

    Worry can be of assistance when we are being observant of our surroundings and acting on our awareness of unusual behavior. Worry can also lead us to effective planning. Estate planning and financial diversification is a part of this.

- We learn from it:

    Is it making us sick? Is it uncontrollable? Is it hurting our relationships? Is it leading to depression or obsessive-compulsive tendencies? Do we need to go talk to someone? Is it a stumbling block in our walk in Christ? Is it at the point where it has become sin in our lives?

- It helps performance (to a point) when it relates to what is in our circle of control:

> *The more you worry, the better you do, up to a point. The key is to know how to stop at that point. Too much worry leads to a host of medical complications... (Hallowell, Worry).*

In the Workplace

The irony of anxiety is that it can make us better at what we do before it becomes unhealthy. My bent toward anxiety makes me very good at my job, which requires attention to detail and a certain level of obsessiveness. Plus, I am the owner of the business, which leads to even more attention to detail. My anxiety, although less when I was in my early 20's, made me very good in the military. I was Enlisted of the Year for the Atlantic Intelligence Command and received multiple awards and letters of commendation. Have you evaluated how God has used your bent toward anxiety in a positive way in your work?

In School

My anxiety led me to a 3.9 average for my Associate's Degree in Computer Science, a 3.9 average for my Bachelor's Degree in Organizational Leadership and Management, as well as Undergraduate Student of the Year. Yes, there are many negatives of anxiety, and we want to reduce the useless anxiety to keep ourselves healthy, but we can also make the most of the anxiety within areas of control: work, grades, and our relationship with Christ.

Parenting

Raising kids is hard. The heaviness of the responsibility is not lost on most parents. We want to do our best and that can lead to a lot of additional anxiety. I don't know how parents who don't have a relationship with Christ manage it. My anxiety is constantly leading me to try and take care of it all on my own and then, when common sense kicks in, I lift up my care to God.

I homeschooled my children, and my anxiety worked for me in the beginning. I made sure everything was done correctly per the requirements of the state. They learned what they needed to learn, in far fewer hours than public school, and they were ahead of the curve in all areas. It only got harder when they were teenagers, when I wasn't able to emotionally handle their teenage angst and pushback. Thankfully, it all worked out, and I am glad I followed through with it. But the stress always makes my anxiety worse, and without the blessing of medication, I would not have been able to raise healthy, smart, and "normal" children.

Purpose

> *For a Christian, anxiety is one of the most powerful opportunities for [spiritual] transformation we'll ever encounter (Curtis Chang).*

Find a way to transform your anxiety into your purpose. If we use it, then we will be less likely to wallow in it and share it with others ad nauseam. We can find ways to make it an opportunity: helping others through it or channeling it into projects. Take your strengths and weave in your weaknesses to create something that is uniquely you. The things we are trying to reject about ourselves may be the exact things God is trying to use to work through us.

Obviously, writing this book is one of the ways I try and help others with anxiety and it also reminds me of important truths that I can easily forget in my daily circumstances: God's sovereignty, God's love for me, and that I am not less because I need something more like medication.

Maybe you play an instrument, write poems, write songs, paint, craft, or do sports. Whatever your talent is, how can you use your struggle with anxiety to help others? Perhaps your anxiety can lead you to improve in these talents and skills? When I am struggling emotionally, it is very helpful to get out of my head and go work on a project. Let your anxiety be a trigger to push you into a project when there is nothing within your circle of control to do.

It is very possible that your anxiety may be the catalyst God uses to put you on track for a purpose you never imagined. This is why we can stay hopeful. He is working in ways we cannot see.

Now to Him who is able to do immeasurably more than all we ask or imagine, according to His power that is at work within us (Ephesians 3:20).

~ Chapter 10 ~
Anger

Consider it pure joy, my brothers and sisters, whenever you face trials of many kinds, because you know that the testing of your faith produces perseverance (James 1:2-3).

Dear Anxious Christian,

The only emotion that seems more powerful than anxiety in my life is anger. I am amazed at the power of it:
- My energy is boosted (I can walk or run longer and faster).
- I won't speak a word (which is amazing!).
- I clean aggressively (and I hate cleaning).

Of course, the result of my anger is usually more negative:
- I think irrationally, negatively, or with all or nothing thinking.
- I try and escape in some way to avoid confrontation.
- I can hold my anger for a very long time.
- I swear.

Just like our anxiety can reach a point of sin, so can anger. Therefore, anger is not a sin in itself. It is what we do with it that brings sin into the picture. I am fully aware of my triggers when it comes to anger. Are you? For example, I get very angry if I am made to feel stupid or embarrassed. I get furious if

I am not aware of something in my own business and then find out in some obscure way (which is another form of embarrassment). Knowing what sets us off is the first step to dealing with the problem of anger.

My anger level is also directly tied to my anxiety level. It is WAY worse when I am off medication; I cannot look at a situation logically or detached. My family is also very aware of this fact. Which is why, when I am off medication, I tell my immediate family and employees. They are more patient with me.

Thankfully, there are many great resources for Christians when it comes to anger. You don't know what's in you until you are squeezed. That's where trials and how we react to them teaches us a lot about ourselves.

Words

Fools give full vent to their rage, but the wise bring calm in the end (Proverbs 29:11).

Anger is a common emotion, but uncontrolled anger can cause life changing problems. Anger can hinder our prayers, make us sick, and ruin relationships. When we are hurt, we tend to hurt others with our angry words. We rarely go to God first and talk through it with Him.

Repeating our hurts over and over to anyone who will listen just creates bitterness from that anger. The faster we can solve issues, the better off everyone will be. Bitterness steals our joy and peace. For our emotional health, we need to forgive others and ourselves; it is an attribute of the strong.

My relationship with my brother has been awful for more than twenty years. He and I never sat down and talked about the concerns and anger that was underlying every conversation. Perhaps if we did, we would be friends today. But both of us have a serious anger streak blended with stubbornness. God has worked on this area in my life for years, and I am happy to say that I try not to say anything negative or hurtful, if I have an opportunity to say anything at all.

Unfortunately, I'm not always successful at this. Therefore, I often need to have other people read my words before I say or send them to hear what message is being expressed. I continually need to check my attitude and heart when it comes to this relationship. For my health, have I truly forgiven him, and am I praying for him? It's hard to hate and pray for someone at the same time.

> *In your anger do not sin: Do not let the sun go down while you are still angry, and do not give the devil a foothold (Ephesians 4:26-27).*
>
> *Sin is not ended by multiplying words, but the prudent hold their tongues (Proverbs 10:19).*

Trials

> *Learn that all that comes into your life, even those irritating discouragements with others, is sent of the Lord, either to reveal something in your own heart that you haven't seen or to give you an opportunity to manifest the sweet reasonableness of the Lord Jesus (Ray Stedman).*

It is the meaning we give to the circumstances and events in our life that lead to our emotional reactions. It all begins with our thoughts. The value and meaning we give to these situations initiates our anger and other emotions. It is not the situation, event, or circumstance itself that is doing it.

Set your minds on things above, not on earthly things (Colossians 3:2).

Thinking Christ-like doesn't come automatically. It requires fighting for it. It requires immersion in God's Word and seeking His wisdom in all situations. And the fight begins long before circumstances occur.

Fight the good fight of the faith. Take hold of the eternal life to which you were called when you made your good confession in the presence of many witnesses (1 Timothy 6:12).

The fight for peace and emotional health begins with being habitual with our God-time. Studying scripture and memorizing it. Reading books about God's Word that will give us greater insight. In this way, we are better equipped to handle the trials and tribulations that come. We are also more likely to be successful at being thankful for them. In fact, it is God who is changing us gradually according to His timing as we put our trust and faith in Him.

And we all, who with unveiled faces contemplate the Lord's glory, are being transformed into his image with ever-increasing glory, which comes from the Lord, who is the Spirit (2 Corinthians 3:18).

Consequences

There are always going to be consequences to our outbursts of anger, and we should never make decisions in the midst of an episode. It is far better to wait for those emotions to subside before doing anything. Even better: be sure you have God's peace about it before you act. I love that we can bring everything to Him, even the small things, because everything is small to Him.

Ironically, it is often the pain and suffering I put on myself from the impulsive, anger outburst that ends up being worse than whatever made me angry in the first place. We unnecessarily heap shame and guilt on ourselves when we react in our anger.

Reframing

> ***Consider it pure joy, my brothers and sisters, whenever you face trials of many kinds, because you know that the testing of your faith produces perseverance. Let perseverance finish its work so that you may be mature and complete, not lacking anything (James 1:2-4).***

Reframing is an excellent way to help with anxiety and anger. It also helps us understand others when we can see a situation in a different light. We have to change the way we think about our family, friends, work, etc. Then we will change the way we act.

Complaining is usually our first go-to for problems. We need to take our complaints and develop a vision and plan to fix anything that is within our circle of control. Our thoughts and how we process them are something we can definitely control or, at the very least, improve gradually each year until it becomes automatic. Our trials produce patience in us, especially when we find joy in them. This is where reframing comes into play. We need to ignore the "thorns" of a situation and instead see the "roses." Paul had to learn the secret of being content. It did not come naturally for him. This should give us an additional glimmer of hope into our own lives.

> *I know what it is to be in need, and I know what it is to have plenty. I have learned the secret of being content in any and every situation, whether well fed or hungry, whether living in plenty or in want (Philippians 4:12).*

Our bad days help us appreciate our good days. Our bad times reveal the awesomeness of our good times. We grow mentally and spiritually during the hard times, as we continue to make God the center of those situations. All the trials, events, and situations are a part of who we are inside and are working for our good because of our love for God and His love for us.

> *...In all these things we are more than conquerors through Him who loved us (Romans 8:37).*

Triggers

We all have an idea of what gets us upset. When I am off my medication, I have a list of items that I know will cause me to flip out in either anger or sadness. I have tracked them over time and know which ones are the hardest. If I have multiple triggers, it can completely immobilize me.

Some of my triggers can be every day activities that another person can handle with no problem. Other triggers are offenses and fear. I take these triggers and dig deep with God to try and figure out what is going on in my head when these situations happen. Remember, we can and should take everything to Him so we can grow from these experiences. We never want to stay where we are...the goal is to grow in wisdom. The most important thing we can do in regard to triggers is to not let them pile up. Dealing with each one as it comes will help with the overwhelming feelings.

My life verse is Romans 12:1-2. It reminds me to give my all in my journey to be a faithful follower of Christ, and to trust that His Word renews me whenever I am reading it:

> ***Therefore, I urge you, brothers and sisters, in view of God's mercy, to offer your bodies as a living sacrifice, holy and pleasing to God—this is your true and proper worship. Do not conform to the pattern of this world, but be transformed by the renewing of your mind. Then you will be able to test and approve what God's will is—His good, pleasing and perfect will (Romans 12:1-2).***

I encourage you to choose verses that you can memorize and apply during difficult moments (triggers) for your anxiety. Triggers can come in all shapes and sizes: unfairness, favoritism, rejection, not being informed or updated. One of my triggers is getting bad news in the mail and not being able to do anything about it. So, I don't check the mail after 4pm or on the weekends. For me, ignorance is bliss in this area. It can wait until Monday.

Another trigger for anger is burnout. If we let ourselves get overwhelmed and pressured, we can let that frustration build up and then overflow onto our loved ones. We also have to evaluate if we are putting too much pressure on ourselves. Taking a look at what we are expecting from ourselves can help us see if we are unnecessarily making our lives more difficult. Check your to-do list and go over it with God. Has He put all the items on there? Remember: Jesus rested. He lived a balanced life. That should be our goal as well.

Be still before the Lord and wait patiently for Him (Psalm 37:7a).

But those who hope in the Lord will renew their strength. They will soar on wings like eagles; they will run and not grow weary, they will walk and not be faint (Isaiah 40:31).

~ Chapter 11 ~
Study & Scriptures

When I am afraid, I put my trust in you (Psalm 56:3).

Dear Anxious Christian,

Many years ago, I completed a Bible study on marriage that changed how I did my God-time forever. It was exactly what I needed to get into specific Scriptures and learn more by digging deep. The method is excellent, and I used it daily for years. There is so much potential for discovery and revelation in the method, which I layout below.

The 5 "P" Method:

Note: This method is highlighted in the workbook Living God's Word *by Waylon B. Moore, but it is now out of print. Older, used copies can be found online.*

First: Choose a Scripture and write it down.
Second: Follow the below steps:

1) **Perimeter:** Read before and after the verse and write down what is happening around it to gain context.
2) **Paraphrase:** Take the verse with the perimeter in mind and put the verse into your own words.

3) **Pulverize:** Pick a word and break the verse down around it by WHO, WHAT, WHERE, WHEN, WHY, and HOW questions. (I then put the details into a new version of the verse.)
4) **Personalize:** How does this verse impact you and what is going on in your life?
5) **Prayer:** Take the verse to God and write down a prayer revolving around it.

Here is an example of one of my entries using this method.

His divine power has given us everything we need for a godly life through our knowledge of Him who called us by his own glory and goodness (2 Peter 1:3).

- **Perimeter**: (This verse is at the opening of the letter, so a study Bible helps put the opening verses into perspective.) Peter is writing to Christians (likely in Asia Minor) and Peter is probably at the end of his life. Christians in Asia Minor were surrounded by Gnostic thinking, which is a form of dualism where everything spiritual is good and everything earthly is bad.
- **Paraphrase:** God, in all His power, has given me all I need right now to live with a genuine reverence toward Him, so I can govern my attitude toward everything in my life through my knowledge of Him who called me via the excellence of His being and His excellence expressed in deeds.
- **Pulverize:**
  - Word=Knowledge
  - Who=God
  - What=Gives

- Where=My heart
- When=Ask God
- Why=He loves me
- How=Goodness

   God gives my heart knowledge when I ask Him via His goodness because He loves me.

- **Personalize:** Do I ask God for increased wisdom and knowledge? It comes only from Him.
- **Prayer:** I know you, God, because You have called me. I have everything I need to live each day in godliness. You call me, who is undeserving and fallen, to be in your Kingdom. I ask that you would increase my knowledge and wisdom, and that I would apply it where necessary to share the love of your Son with the lost. In Jesus' name, Amen.

I hope you can discover the joy of this method. Here are some more of my own examples with anxiety related verses.

Cast all your anxiety on Him because He cares for you (1 Peter 5:7).

- **Perimeter**: Humble yourself. Do not be proud.
- **Paraphrase:** Throw (get rid of, toss) God all your anger, care, worries, and anxieties because He cares for you.
- **Pulverize:**
  - Word=Anxiety
  - Who=Belongs to God
  - What=Not meant for me to hold
  - Where=Throw Him the concerns
  - When=They are out of my control
  - Why=Because He can handle them
  - How=By giving them over to Him in prayer

I can throw God all my anxiety wrapped in prayer, which I was never meant to hold when out of my control, because He can handle them and they belong to Him.

- **Personalize:** I will cast all my care upon God because He cares for me.
- **Prayer:** Father, this verse can be so hard to follow, yet it is so simple. I continue to hold on to anxieties that I should be lifting up to you continually. Help me to throw you all the cares that try to consume me.

Search me, Oh God, and know my heart; try me, and know my anxieties; and see if there is any wicked way in me, and lead main the way everlasting (Psalm 139:23.24).

- **Perimeter**: God knows my words, thoughts, and inner being. He knows my motives better than I know myself.
- **Paraphrase:** Look within me, Lord, and know the details of my heart. Test me in my worries and fears. Guide me into Christlikeness.
- **Pulverize:**
    - Word=Know
    - Who=God
    - What=Everything
    - Where=In the heart
    - When=In actions
    - Why=He is everlasting
    - How=By forming me
        God knows everything in my heart, including my actions, because He formed me and is everlasting.
- **Personalize:** God searches me, and He knows my heart. He tries me and knows the areas I struggle with. He can

see if there is any area within me that must be led into truth.
- **Prayer:** Father, I am so glad you know what anxieties are within me and the struggles that I am going through concerning them. Please continue to work within me in this area. I pray that my struggles are helpful to others and that our relationship grows closer and closer until we meet face to face.

Scripture List

Below are the Scriptures, by chapter and order, featured in the book. I encourage you to take a deep dive into each one using the above method or a method of your choosing that enhances your study. I would love to hear how the book and the Scriptures are of help and revelation in your life. Contact info is at the end of the book.

1: Is My Anxiety a Disorder
- ☐ John 14:16
- ☐ John 8:31-32
- ☐ 1 Corinthians 1:27
- ☐ 1 Peter 5:7
- ☐ Proverbs 16:9
- ☐ 2 Corinthians 10:4-5
- ☐ Mark 5:36

2: Circumstantial Anxiety is Different
- ☐ Galatians 6:7
- ☐ Galatians 6:9
- ☐ Psalm 55:22
- ☐ Romans 9:18
- ☐ Psalm 77:11
- ☐ Philippians 4:6

- ☐ 1 John 4:18
- ☐ Mark 11:24

3: God Knows and Cares
- ☐ Hebrews 4:15-16
- ☐ Proverbs 12:25
- ☐ Psalm 94:19
- ☐ Romans 14:4
- ☐ Matthew 7:3-5
- ☐ Ephesians 4:32
- ☐ Philippians 4:13
- ☐ Romans 12:21
- ☐ Matthew 5:48
- ☐ Philippians 3:12-14
- ☐ Psalm 88:3-4
- ☐ Matthew 19:26
- ☐ Proverbs 3:7
- ☐ Philippians 4:8-9

4: Self-Reflection
- ☐ Philippians 4:6
- ☐ John 16:33
- ☐ Philippians 4:7
- ☐ Proverbs 29:25
- ☐ Zephaniah 3:16b-17
- ☐ Philippians 1:6
- ☐ Matthew 6:21

5: Daily Living
- ☐ Joshua 1:5
- ☐ James 5:16
- ☐ Ephesians 4:2
- ☐ Psalm 139:1-2
- ☐ James 5:12
- ☐ Romans 8:28
- ☐ Colossians 3:15

- ☐ John 14:1
- ☐ 1 Peter 5:7
- ☐ Psalm 55:22
- ☐ Matthew 11:28
- ☐ Isaiah 26:3
- ☐ 1 Peter 5:8
- ☐ Psalm 46:10
- ☐ 2 Timothy 1:7
- ☐ Deuteronomy 8:2
- ☐ John 3:29b-30

6: Have a Talk with Yourself

- ☐ Proverbs 29:18
- ☐ Proverbs 14:30
- ☐ Proverbs 13:10
- ☐ John 14:27
- ☐ 2 Corinthians 10:5

7: Accepting the Less Than Perfect Days

- ☐ Psalm 73:26
- ☐ Psalm 34:18
- ☐ Jeremiah 29:11
- ☐ Proverbs 3:5-6
- ☐ John 6:28-29
- ☐ John 14:17
- ☐ Psalm 69:30
- ☐ Hebrews 12:2
- ☐ Isaiah 43:19
- ☐ Hebrews 10:17
- ☐ Philippians 2:14
- ☐ 1 Thessalonians 5:16-19
- ☐ Philippians 2:21

8: Relationships

- ☐ Galatians 5:22-23
- ☐ Colossians 3:23-24

- ☐ Ephesians 4:29
- ☐ 1 Thessalonians 5:11a
- ☐ Ephesians 6:12

9: Positives of Anxiety
- ☐ 2 Corinthians 4:17
- ☐ Luke 22:39-44
- ☐ Matthew 6:27
- ☐ Matthew 6:34
- ☐ Matthew 6:21
- ☐ Ephesians 3:20

10: Anger
- ☐ James 1:2-3
- ☐ Proverbs 29:11
- ☐ Ephesians 4:26-27
- ☐ Proverbs 10:19
- ☐ Colossians 3:2
- ☐ 1 Timothy 6:12
- ☐ 2 Corinthians 3:18
- ☐ James 1:2-4
- ☐ Philippians 4:12
- ☐ Romans 8:37
- ☐ Romans 12:1-2
- ☐ Psalm 37:7a
- ☐ Isaiah 40:31

11: Study & Scriptures
- ☐ Psalm 56:3

120

~ Chapter 12 ~
# My Anxiety Testimony

Dear Anxious Christian,

Before coming to Christ when I was 24, I knew I had more anxiety than the normal person. Normal people don't cry for months in kindergarten, freak out at the age of six when they can't go to school, or imagine death and accidents when someone is twenty minutes late. (Although, our own death has been called the "ultimate worry.") Anxiety was normal for me, and perfectionism and the fear of failure grew over time.

But debilitating anxiety and excessive anger were not a part of my life—to the extent that it hurt my relationships—until my life got complicated. As I looked back in my journals in preparation for this book, I believe that my mental health declined exponentially due to stress.

When I came to Christ, I had a wonderful job as a Naval Systems Analyst—a job I easily got due to my previous job experience while active in the Navy. I was a newlywed who just bought her first home. I was going to school full time in an advanced degree program, and I loved it. Yet, it was not the full-time job, full-time schooling, and an active life that began my decline: it was what I stacked on top of those things.

My husband and I started a home-based business and worked it in the evenings. It was very slow at first and easy enough for us to handle. The stress of starting the business, handling the paperwork, doing the accounting, and building the website were the obvious next steps to my mental overload. I have heard stress described as living out of balance, and I agree that it can be a good indicator.

My journals show how overwhelmed I was becoming at work and at home. Yet I was so thankful for what God was doing. I was also active in my church's choir, the praise team, and blessed with great parts in all the dramas at Christmas and Easter; just a few other activities on top of all that was going on.

We got two wonderful dogs and my husband had to travel more with work, which left me doing everything at home. I also started volunteering as a Friend to the Elderly by visiting specific residents at nursing homes.

At that time, I started suffering from more frequent mouth ulcers and sicknesses. Most of my family detested my faith in Christ, and they were not shy about sharing their feelings. This added another dimension of stress to my life.

And then, like many women in their later 20's, I started desiring children. I was pregnant two months later. But nothing came off my calendar; I didn't back down from any activities. In fact, I worked until two days before my first son was born, I continued my degree, I played the lead in the drama at church, and did financial work for the business at night.

Surprisingly, my journal only occasionally mentioned my anxiety. Before my son was born, I started a new drama ministry at church and became the lead on numerous weapons systems at work. Pregnancy did not slow me down. Giving birth did.

I had an emergency c-section and almost lost my little boy. He was born during Christmas, and I had little help with breastfeeding. Everything was closed.

Over the next two months, I suffered from infections and disappointment, yet I kept up with the paperwork and even switched accounting software (a major project). I prepared to go back to work.

The search for daycare was exhausting, and I was starting to feel led to stay home. But I had an amazing and well-paying job. Only a stupid person would quit. So, I stayed on and suppressed my feelings.

My hormones, my stress, and my body fell deeper into harmful moments of anxiety.

If all this wasn't enough, we bought a very nice boat, and placed it two hours away in a beautiful lake. That was an eye-opening moment into my anxiety. I worried about everything. Ridiculous things. Unlikely things. All things.

When I was forced to change daycare providers when my son was eight months old, my urge to stay home was too strong and we agreed it was time. The home-business was doing well, although not in any way able to make up for the money I was giving up at my job, and the desire to stay home was undeniable. We agreed it was time for me to quit my job. Everyone thought I was crazy. My company was so disappointed in me.

Taking care of a home, a baby, and a business took its toll. I stopped doing all the things I enjoyed including my time with God, except for weekend services. My college classes were still ongoing—I never took a break after I gave birth. The stress led to weight loss and then to sickness. I was practically bedridden for two months. Looking back, I can see that stress was moving me from a level of "functional anxiety" into a dysfunctional state.

After I got better physically, I went back to all my normal activities. This lifestyle of elevated stress and anxiety lasted for a couple years.

My journals reflect that I was happy and constantly thankful for what God had given me. However, the entries began to show doubt as a mom, a wife, and as a disciple. I begin to assume the negative about most things—mostly about myself. When my son was one, I wrote this in my journal:

> *More and more people are suggesting I consider going on medication for my anxiousness. I must admit I have thought about it. But I feel it would be the wrong step for a number of reasons: 1) I want another baby. 2) I fear it makes me a failure. 3) I am concerned it will change my personality. But at the same time, my panic attacks have been increasing and I feel I can't control these thoughts.*

I didn't mention it in the entry, but I also did not want my mom to be right since she always felt like I needed medication (she always thought I was bi-polar and did not agree with the diagnosis of GAD). Although my weight was still considerably too low, and I was exhausted all the time, I wanted another baby and I didn't not want to be on medication during that time. I was pregnant a few months later.

My stress and hormones continued to cause a decline in my mental health. I was more depressed for significant no reason. I had fits of rage over the smallest things. Everything was large and magnified. Offenses, irritations, and the imperfections of others and myself were triggers of emotional instability.

I also began to resent what I was initially drawn to in my husband: his stable, calm, and peaceful nature. I hated that he didn't get angry or sad. I began to resent the business we created, as it took a lot of time away from being with my son (even in the same home) and limited other activities I could have been doing.

My relationship with my non-Christian family was further declining, and I felt their silent judgement of me: aren't Christians supposed to be joyful, loving, and kind? But it was not my faith that was the problem, it was my stress. And the hormones from my pregnancy were not helping. I brought my aches and cares to God daily:

Anger, God. It pours from me all the time as of late. I have horrible thoughts about my life. I do and think things that I don't want to do or think. I'm sad, upset, frustrated. I am tired of feeling down and depressed over not having time to be the perfect everything. I need you, Lord. I need more of You in me.

I graduated at the top of my class and received my bachelor's degree and took up more quilting projects, drama parts at church, and joined a Bible study with some neighbors to fill in the time school had taken. My husband began being honest and vocal about my negativity, offense, and anger. I was often blowing up and then apologizing. It was a horrible cycle.

Our business was booming and our second son would arrive soon, but I needed help (finally, some common sense in the stress department).

We decided that my husband would quit his fantastic job and we would move to Ohio with our home-based business and let my mother-in-law help with the boys during the week so I could work the business and have some time to relax. There was nothing tying us down to our location since our business was internet-based. People thought my husband was crazy, but we knew God had called me to quit my job years before and He was calling my husband now to quit his. But before leaving, and at seven months pregnant, we endured an unexpected trial that led my husband to see an opportunity:

we started a second online business. Cue more paperwork and worry for me.

My resentment with him grew and I fought with him more.

Father, I am stressing a lot. I am completely overwhelmed and tired. I'm longing for quiet time and not getting into stupid arguments. There is so much work to do.

My second son was born in the midst of searching for homes. When he was two months old, we moved to our new home in Ohio and put our other home on the market. Side note: buying a home, selling a home, and moving to that home while having and caring for a baby and a toddler is madness.

Father, I feel unable to breathe with all the pressure. I feel like I am going to have a breakdown.

One would think my stress would have been less after the move, but it continued. And it got worse. I started new projects. I became part of new ministries and worked the additional business. But I tried hard to apply what I learned in college: prioritize.

In all honesty, I am leaving out so many activities and events that only added to my stress and decline—and quite a few that brought great happiness and joy. I aim only to paint a picture of my nature (I love to be active and do things) and my conflict (I can't do it all).

After a couple years, I became sick again. I ate horribly and couldn't relax at all. My body began fighting itself with extreme inflammation that would be a continuous problem in my life. My boys were thriving, our businesses were booming, but my mental health was about to hit rock bottom if I did not do something. And soon, my marriage would reach the point where action was required if it was to stay intact.

It was time to put my pride and perfectionism aside and address the problem; I went to my primary care physician. He had always seen me as self-assured and confident. This appointment was different. I couldn't stop crying. I told him I was praying, reading about reducing my anxiety, exercising, and doing everything that was supposed to help relieve it with no success. He asked me about my family's mental health and we agreed that I would start a very low dose of generic Paxil, the same medication that my mother took that seemed to work for her.

Three days later everything and nothing changed. My circumstances remained unchanged yet my emotions were the most stable they had been in years. I was sitting down and watching TV without worrying or jumping up and down to get tasks done. I was stunned. My husband was amazed. He called the next eight months the "honeymoon phase."

The dosage was so small it wasn't even supposed to be able to do anything, yet it did. I wrote in my journal:

I can finally apply all the techniques for reducing worry and anxiety I have read about all these years. I am not fighting without cause with my husband, and I am able to better tolerate people who are different from me. Thank you so much, Lord.

The peace was unbelievable. Within seven months, however, the messages I was hearing from the pulpit were heavy on trusting God for healing and getting off medication. I felt a load of guilt for being on it. I hate that I listened to those words and let them get into my head, but I did. I went off the medication, with the blessing of my husband, to see if I was able to move forward without debilitating anxiety.

I did feel like generic Paxil gave me a view of what peace looked like. Maybe I could mimic it without the meds. Within three weeks, I was in a big fight with a family member, I was talking about my problems too much, and I was a strain on my marriage again. I began losing weight and getting sick. The honeymoon was over.

And so here began the cycle that would continue for the next two decades: go off medication, try, struggle, go back on medication, feel peace, feel guilt, go off medication...

My months and years of being on medication were longer than being off meds, so my life was relatively balanced emotionally. The years I was off meds were, unfortunately, so hard that they are etched into my memory and the memories of my family.

It is clear that my mental and physical health are better on meds than off. I am easier to get along with and I enjoy life more. Therefore, I am very open and honest with all my friends and family about the situation and they are extra patient with me. I make sure that I do my due diligence to monitor my emotions and have a person (sponsor) I can go to and work through issues as they occur.

I have to constantly fight a plethora of feelings about my anxiety: guilt for being off meds and making my family's life more difficult, anger for being a better me on meds than off, irritation that I can't handle more stressful events in my life without all these emotions, etc.

Truly accepting myself, I think, is a lifelong journey of trusting God and reminding myself of His love for me. He knows exactly who I am (He created me) and knows what I struggle with every day. He is a good, good Father who encourages me and shares the hard truths with me that I probably don't want to hear. But He does it in such a way as to remind me that He's got me in the palm of His hand.

And I must remind myself, and maybe you, dear reader, that even on meds God still loves us. I will struggle with failure and with guilt. But I must remember: He is an understanding Daddy, and He is not mad at me.

He is not mad at you either.

He loves you.

Word Find

(Find the capitalized words listed on the next page.)

C	Z	G	V	H	B	T	H	B	Y	T	J	V	G	Q
W	I	S	D	O	M	R	F	D	G	E	K	N	O	W
K	M	N	J	H	B	V	G	I	C	G	X	D	D	A
B	U	X	Q	N	J	L	G	T	L	K	V	M	E	Y
V	N	B	G	W	R	S	P	I	R	I	T	C	L	T
O	F	Z	H	T	K	T	T	M	B	R	P	X	K	E
N	A	G	K	U	R	W	X	Q	A	E	F	N	F	I
U	I	V	K	A	S	U	A	N	C	N	H	W	K	X
O	L	N	E	B	H	K	S	G	T	E	C	P	T	N
W	I	H	H	F	W	F	X	T	J	W	K	N	V	A
K	N	V	B	P	O	W	Q	R	S	I	A	N	B	W
Y	G	M	N	R	Q	V	C	M	I	N	D	L	R	T
C	Z	Y	M	N	C	S	L	Q	Z	G	A	N	Z	C
G	F	E	A	R	O	U	W	N	W	H	C	K	U	P
S	D	M	N	O	F	R	K	M	N	C	P	W	L	G
L	J	G	H	K	C	S	C	Q	I	U	W	O	R	D
P	O	Q	N	B	Z	T	O	E	V	S	V	N	B	Z
D	C	A	R	E	S	I	R	Q	O	E	M	Y	A	X
U	H	N	V	Y	U	F	O	R	E	V	E	R	E	P
T	P	X	E	W	M	I	A	S	O	U	L	B	C	N

I will not ☐FEAR.

I will ☐TRUST in You.

You are my ☐ROCK, ☐LORD.

I am ☐TRANSFORMED by ☐RENEWING my ☐MIND.

☐WISDOM is found Your ☐WORD.

☐GOD, You have, and will always, ☐LOVE me.

Thank you for your ☐UNFAILING love.

I am so ☐THANKFUL for your ☐SPIRIT within me.

You ☐KNOW the ☐ANXIETY that has consumed me.

I can ☐LIFT all my ☐CARES up to you.

You know my ☐HEART and my ☐SOUL.

☐FOREVER I am yours. Amen.

References

Anderson, N. T. & Miller, R. (1999). *Freedom from fear: Overcoming worry & anxiety*. Harvest House.

Burns, D. D. (1980). *Feeling good: The new mood therapy*. HarperCollins.

Chang, C. (2023). *The anxiety opportunity: How worry is the doorway to your best self*. Zondervan.

Hallowell, E M. (1997). *Worry: Controlling it and using it wisely*. Random House.

Lewis, C. S. (1952). *Mere Christianity*. Geoffrey Bless.

Moore, W. B. (1997). *Living God's Word: Practical lessons for applying Scripture to life*. Lifeway Press.

Moreland, J. P. (2019). *Finding quiet: My story of overcoming anxiety and the practices that brought peace*. Zondervan.

Neff, K. (2015). *Self-compassion*. William Morrow Paperbacks.

Simpson, A. (2015). *Let God change your mind*. In Touch Ministries. https://www.intouch.org/read/articles/let-god-change-your-mind

Stedman, R. (1963). *Standing while running.* https://www.raystedman.org/new-testament/philippians/standing-while-running

Stedman, R. (1986). *Where hope begins.* https://www.raystedman.org/new-testament/colossians/where-hope-begins

Swindoll, C. (2012). *Living the proverbs.* Worthy Publishing.

Connect

Website: www.LillyHorigan.com
E-Mail: info@LillyHorigan.com
Via Snail Mail: Lilly Books, PO Box 223, Bolivar, OH, 44612

About the Author

Lilly lives in Bolivar, Ohio, with her husband and two boys. She is originally from Horseheads, New York.

Other Books by Lilly

Paper Treasures

Paper Treasures is Lilly's first inspirational novel based on true events. Published 2019.

Paige McKinnon has finally graduated high school and is ready to embark on the journey she has been planning for years. Alone, she makes her way to Las Vegas where she hopes to locate her mentally ill and homeless mother. A young woman of faith, Paige uses only the prompting of God's Spirit and advice of her aunt to find a place to stay, work, and search for her mother's whereabouts—but will she find love there as well?

Does Everything Happen for a Reason, God?

Lilly's first devotional: *Does Everything Happen for a Reason, God?* Published 2020.

This devotional is packed with God's Word and the wisdom of strong biblical scholars to help answer this common question while discovering purpose and God's sovereignty amidst the situations in our own lives.

Your Mommy Was Little Too

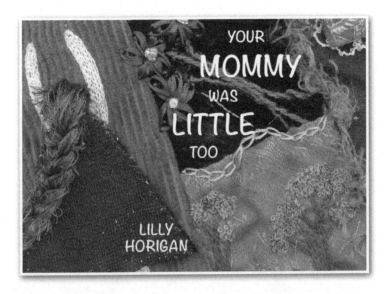

Lilly's first children's book: *Your Mommy Was Little Too.* Published 2020.

Children have a hard time imagining their parents as kids. Lilly's Christian children's book shares how a mommy played and dreamed, and how God made her dreams come true with her little one. Lilly has filled this book with her own thread art and reminds the reader that God is the great Creator. Throughout the book there are learning activities, Bible verses, and encouragement for parents. This book is for ideal for children ages 3-8.

Shimmering One

Lilly's first short story: *Shimmering One.* Published 2021.

When eleven-year-old Emily walks down her street, she passes by a woman who is always sitting on her porch—day after day. The summer passes, yet the porch lady remains. Until, one day, she doesn't. The missing woman is a mystery that will only be solved with time and the help of one of God's wondrous creations.